The Power of Groups

The Power of Groups

of

Groups

Solution-Focused Group
Counseling in Schools

LESLIE COOLEY

CORWIN
A SAGE Company

For information:

Corwin
A SAGE Company
2455 Teller Road
Thousand Oaks, California 91320
(800) 233-9936
Fax: (800) 417-2466
www.corwinpress.com

SAGE Ltd.
1 Oliver's Yard
55 City Road
London EC1Y 1SP
United Kingdom

SAGE India Pvt. Ltd.
B 1/I 1 Mohan Cooperative
 Industrial Area
Mathura Road,
 New Delhi 110 044
India

SAGE Asia-Pacific Pte. Ltd.
33 Pekin Street #02-01
Far East Square
Singapore 048763

Printed in the United States of America.

Library of Congress Cataloging-in-Publication Data

Cooley, Leslie.
The power of groups: solution-focused group counseling in schools/Leslie Cooley.
    p. cm.
Includes bibliographical references and index.
ISBN 978-1-4129-7096-9 (cloth)
ISBN 978-1-4129-7097-6 (pbk.)
    1. Group guidance in education. 2. School psychology. I. Title.

LB1027.55.C68 2009
371.4′047—dc22   2008053487

This book is printed on acid-free paper.

13 14 15 16 17 10 9 8 7 6 5 4 3 2

Acquisitions Editor:	Jessica Allan
Editorial Assistant:	Joanna Coelho
Production Editor:	Libby Larson
Copy Editor:	Jenifer Dill
Typesetter:	C&M Digitals (P) Ltd.
Proofreader:	Theresa Kay
Indexer:	Terri Corry
Cover Designer:	Michael Dubowe

Contents

Preface

WHY SHOULD YOU READ THIS BOOK?

You should read this book if you

- would like to learn how to be an effective group leader using a solution-focused approach to group counseling,
- are just beginning your career and would like to learn processes that will make setting up and leading groups much easier,
- are an experienced leader and would like to increase the probability that your group counseling meetings go as planned, perhaps even exceeding your expectations,
- would like to avoid spending time ensnared in the many pitfalls common to inexperienced group leaders,
- want ideas on handling situations that trip you up,
- are looking for new strategies that will help you do what you set out to do in the first place—positively impact the lives of students.

In addition to teaching new skills, the lessons learned in this book will likely make leading school groups more enjoyable; building on strengths and bringing out the best in students is inherently rewarding. If there has been a lag between the last group you led and the next one you will lead, this book will introduce some exciting new ideas and refresh some helpful old ones. The net effect will be an increase in confidence in your skills.

For both new and experienced practitioners, this book will be a valuable resource—not as a book of activities but, rather, as a companion book to your favorite group counseling or activity books. You will learn to modify activities using a solution-focused approach as the foundation, to create more lively and engaging group meetings, and most important, to promote change in the lives of the students you serve.

WHAT IS HAPPENING TO GROUP COUNSELING?

In 1984, 93 percent of public high schools offered "group guidance/counseling sessions"; in 2002, that number dropped to 85 percent (Parsad, Alexander, Farris, & Hudson, 2004). What is happening? When practitioners were surveyed, the lack of sufficient time for group counseling was the most frequent reason cited (Steen, Bauman, & Smith, 2007). Counselors and others who have offered groups in the past now have multiple obligations, including increased involvement with standardized testing, special education responsibilities, and dealing with behavior management issues.

It is, however, possible that the time crunch cited by counselors is masking other issues. LaFountain's (1993) statewide survey of school counselors examined the relationship between how counselors spend their time and their level of job stress. Job burnout was reported when counselors were asked to perform duties for which they were inadequately trained. One of the areas cited by counselors as an area of inadequate training was group counseling.

Inadequate training in the face of a professional expectation can leave the practitioner in a demoralized position. Failed attempts at group counseling based on weak training can leave the practitioner scrambling for a more familiar and meaningful way to contribute in a school setting. If this accurately describes your experience, this book is a good start at reversing the above trend.

WHY IS THIS BOOK DIFFERENT FROM OTHER BOOKS ON GROUP COUNSELING?

This book specifically addresses two areas of group counseling: (a) how to successfully plan groups in a school setting and (b) how to lead school counseling groups using a solution-focused approach. While books on general group counseling abound, most are collections of group activities and do not have a theoretical orientation or counseling model as a foundation. The typical group counseling book focuses on getting students to talk about their "issues," process what's happening, and share feelings. In contrast, a solution-focused counseling group is strength based: The focus is on goals, what the student wants to do differently, and personal resources. The strategies of a solution-focused approach are consistent with current research on creating change. There is perhaps no better antidote to job burnout than helping to create a positive change in the lives of the students with whom we work.

WHAT WILL I FIND IN THIS BOOK?

An examination of the process of change is a good starting point for any book on counseling. Positive change is, after all, the central issue of all counseling. Chapter 1 is devoted to a discussion of change and the theoretical models that underlie our work with students. Chapter 2 is an examination of the basic assumptions of Solution-Focused Brief Counseling (SFBC) as it relates to groups. In Chapter 3, the techniques and strategies of a solution-focused approach are discussed in the context of group counseling.

The second half of the book has a practical, how-to focus. Chapter 4 begins the conversation on adapting group materials with a discussion of the general principles involved in making group activities consistent with a solution-focused approach. Chapter 5 continues the conversation with specifics on how to take group activities from any curriculum guide and adapt them to be solution focused. Chapter 6 contains a detailed examination of the issues involved in planning and setting up a group. It presents organizational strategies that will set you up for success and make your life easier by helping you actively employ a strength-based approach from the beginning of the process. In Chapter 7, the issues involved in a first meeting are explored, keeping in mind the goal of having a second meeting! We do, after all, want the students to return. Chapter 7 also focuses on how to keep the group going and explores ways to end a group series. In Chapter 8, you will find sample group agendas, with several for elementary, middle, and high school. The focus of Chapter 9 is troubleshooting; the discussion is about things that can go wrong and ways to recover or change direction after they do so. Last, Chapter 10 is a reflection and conclusion. The reader is invited to consider the discussions throughout the book in relation to professional identity and delivering the best possible service to students in the schools.

While getting a counseling group up and running can be challenging, the rewards for both the leader and the participants can be substantial. Most practitioners have some choices about how to serve students. This book will make it easier for you to choose group counseling more often, and it will make you happier with your choice!

Acknowledgments

I am indebted to California State University, Sacramento, for a sabbatical in the spring of 2008. This was the time I needed to write this book, which had been brewing for years.

Several colleagues read drafts of selected chapters and contributed important suggestions for improving the manuscript: Rose Borunda, Steven Koch, Sandi Miller, and Melissa Holland. Their willingness to get involved and share their expertise is greatly appreciated.

My friend Tom Redman provided unending enthusiasm for a project outside of his field. He finished each chapter with the insistence that I send another. It was a delight to share the evolution of this project with him.

My parents are solution focused by nature, so this interest on my part appears to be genetic. I am grateful for their influence on my worldview. While most of my family members cannot recall exactly what this book is about, that has not in any way dampened their interest and support! Hearty thanks to Ann Buckley and Kristine Jensen, who not only gave suggestions on the manuscript but whose lives are filled with strength and resilience.

Vanessa Diffenbaugh was my extraordinary writing coach and personal editor. She added immeasurably to the organization and clarity of this work. She took every moment of mild discouragement and masterfully pointed out everything that was already working . . . a "strength-based" approach that was ideal. I've made it my policy never to write a book without her!

Last, thank you to Corwin and acquisitions editor Jessica Allan, who believed in this idea from the start. I was fortunate to work with production editor Libby Larson, who made the work easy on the eye; editorial assistant Joanna Coelho, who is a master of details; and copy editor Jenifer Dill, who taught me a lot about commas!

I am grateful to the Corwin reviewers who gave helpful direction and feedback as the book took form:

Rhonda Cash
School Psychologist
National School District
National City, CA

Mark Cooksley, MEd
Elementary School Guidance Counselor
Emma Carson Elementary School
Puyallup School District
Puyallup, WA

John Davis
6th Grade Magnet Math and Science Teacher, NBCT
Kittredge Magnet School for High Achievers
Atlanta, GA

Cynthia Knowles
Substance Abuse Prevention Specialist/Consultant
Livonia Central School District
Dansville, NY

Bernita L. Krumm
Assistant Professor
Department of Educational Leadership
College of Education
Oklahoma State University
Stillwater, OK

Sue Ellen McCalley, PhD
Professor
Avila University
Kansas City, MO

Katy Olweilier
Counselor
Lakeside School
Seattle, WA

This project did indeed take a village. . . . Thanks to all who were willing to be in town!

About the Author

 Leslie Cooley worked as a school psychologist in public schools for twenty years. Initially hired in 1978 to facilitate counseling groups, she approached the task with enthusiasm and massive naivety as she had little training in group counseling. Based on her natural optimism and easy way of relating to students, she developed a variety of skills and techniques that were closely related to the later work of the innovators of solution-focused counseling.

That was 1978 through 1983. Since that time, she has earned a PhD and become a licensed clinical psychologist in California. In the 1990s, she transitioned from working in the schools to teaching at the graduate level in school psychology at California State University, Sacramento. Her mission was to surreptitiously infiltrate the school system with what were once radical ideas about building on strengths. In that, she has been successful . . . successfully mainstream! Solution-focused strategies are no longer radical, and books such as Seligman's *Positive Psychology* have become best sellers.

She continues to do a limited psychotherapy practice with a focus on families. And she continues to believe that most of the problems kids develop can be successfully managed at the school level, where any intervention is less intrusive than a referral to someone outside the school.

As a graduate school trainer in school psychology, Dr. Cooley has been teaching group counseling to school psychologists for over a decade. She systematically robs graduate students of the character-building experience that she once had, scrambling to learn to run groups in the schools. However, in the schools today, there is plenty to scramble about already!

To my son, Miles,
whose resilience and vitality are inspiring

CHAPTER ONE

Creating Change One Group at a Time

I n the chapters that follow, your thoughts about how and why we do group counseling may shift. It takes a fair amount of time and planning to set up groups, and you may find yourself wondering if they are worth the extra effort. Why not just see students individually? Wouldn't that be faster in the long run? The pivotal question here is, *Faster for whom?* If the change we seek is more likely to occur in a group setting, then group counseling should be the treatment of choice—anything less is a Band-Aid.

FACILITATING CHANGE

Why start a book on group counseling with a discussion of the theory of change? Change is the quintessence of counseling. It is the raison d'être for being a mental health provider. Our purpose is not mysterious, yet the path for achieving our goal is often elusive. If we can get clear about how we think change occurs, we have a much better chance of making it happen.

How Do You Think Change Occurs?

Whether we realize it or not, our personal theory of change is the driving force behind the actions we take with students. Take a quick inventory of the most common strategies used in the school setting

1

to effect change. We correct misbehavior on the playground with time on the bench and tell kids who cut in line go to the end. When homework is missing, we make calls home and expect parents to "have a word." We ask students if they would like it if someone did that terrible thing to them. Sometimes we give advice to the broken-hearted or console the person always picked last for teams. Some teachers use a classroom "agenda" for grievances and have weekly discussions to repair damages.

Our theory of change in these scenarios involves a simple redirect or punishment. In each case, it is assumed that students will see the merits of our position and, with this new understanding, will make better decisions in the future. Each time we implement one of the above strategies, we have the expectation that the student will see the light, mend their ways, and transform. Well, maybe we just hope they'll *stop it*! But deep down, it is change we are after. Sometimes these strategies work, but often they do not.

If we do the same thing over and over again and expect different results, we are a sure candidate for professional burnout. If we intervene with students and little change occurs, we cease to feel we are contributing to positive change in their lives—the very reason we chose this profession. To avoid this unfortunate cycle and the burnout that will undoubtedly follow, one question is a clear standout. Your answer to this question will rightfully be the underpinning for all the actions you take with students. The question is simple and warrants an informed and deliberate answer: *How do you really think change occurs?*

Take a Look at Your Own Life

In our own lives, we may want to lose ten pounds, have a better relationship with a sibling, or quit a bad habit. Most of us have logged some failed attempts at solving these kinds of recurring problems. From these experiences, we probably know a fair amount about how change does *not* occur. Our response to uninvited lectures and a barrage of "you shoulds" seldom includes a flight into action. More commonly, we become immobilized—even when we know that taking action would be good for us.

We know from our own experience that there is a very low percentage return on lecturing, threatening, withholding, cajoling, persuading, and sharing the dreaded "facts." These tactics do not build relationship or rapport. A casual observation of the typical traffic in and out of the vice principal's office confirms that this approach is ineffective with students as well; students do not respond to lectures, threats, or withholding any better than we do.

Why Groups Help Create Change in Young People

So what does work with students? We know from research and training that group counseling is the treatment of choice for many adolescents; for this demographic, anything a peer says is far more interesting and influential than anything we could say on our best day. Teenagers hang on each others' words, even when they feign indifference. Feedback among teens is usually the fast track to change.

At the elementary level, many of the issues for which students are referred for counseling are social or behavioral in nature. Group counseling is an ideal way to work on the skills necessary to be successful in these areas. We can meet individually with a fifth grader for multiple sessions and practice "not interrupting," but until that behavior is demonstrated repeatedly in a peer group, we cannot say the problem is solved. Group counseling may be a better fit.

Working Within a School System

Take a moment to think about daily life as a practitioner. Many of us who work in schools have had the experience of becoming hypnotized by the school routine. We slog our way down a hefty to-do list and suddenly realize we have forgotten to ask the essential question: *Has anything really changed as a result of my interaction with this student?* Students may be removed from our to-do list once we have seen them individually, but if the issue that brought them to the office would have been better addressed in group counseling, our contribution to a solution may be negligible; our dutiful "checkoff" may be meaningless.

The routine of a school—the way things have always been done—is a force all its own, and it can overcome our good judgment. Too often we are in situations where the fast pace of the environment, the enormous student and family needs, and the time pressure for competing obligations makes group counseling seem like an arduous task and our goal of positively impacting the lives of students with the most effective intervention falls by the wayside. Dedicated professionals are faced with a dilemma: How do we work quickly and efficiently in this fast-paced environment to create situations where genuine change can occur?

As we consider group counseling—and how, when, and why this approach can facilitate change—the starting point is a clear understanding of how change occurs.

AN EQUATION FOR CHANGE

From Asay and Lambert's (1999) research on change, we know that four critical factors combine to promote successful outcomes in counseling. While their research focused on individuals, we can extrapolate as we consider working in groups. If we focus on these interrelated factors, we will maximize our work with students. The four known ingredients of successful and lasting change are discussed below. A fifth ingredient specific to groups is proposed.

Client Factors

Client factors account for 40 percent of change. Client factors are the strengths, talents, resources, gifts, social supports, and values that a student brings with her or him to a group meeting. These assets are the petri dish of change. They may be subtle, embryonic, unevenly developed, or completely unrealized, but they are the strengths that the interactions of the group will nurture. Our goal as group leaders is to make every student's strengths take center stage.

Relationship Factors

Relationship factors account for 30 percent of change. In individual therapy, this is the alliance and perceived support between the practitioner and the participant, and it includes variables such as respect, acceptance, and warmth. In the group setting, relationships are far more complex. The leader has a relationship with each member of the group and with the group as a whole; likewise, each member has the same complex series of relationships with the leader, the other members, and the group. In the group setting, there is a clear need for respect, acceptance, and warmth between the leader and the participants. Because a successful group experience is predicated on members feeling safe and accepted, the challenge for the leader is to develop those same qualities in the group as a whole. Careful planning by the leader (see Chapter 6) is an essential strategy for promoting the kinds of relationships that foster safety, acceptance, and validation; the existence of this kind of environment promotes change. Additional ways to foster positive relationships are discussed in the chapters that follow.

Hope or Expectancy

Hope or expectancy accounts for 15 percent of change. When participants enter counseling, the ability to anticipate that their lives can be different in a desired way is a springboard for change. The fact that hopefulness is not a larger percentage of the change equation, while somewhat unexpected, is perhaps a relief for those of us working in schools. Since students are often referred for counseling services that they might not have chosen, students may lack the qualities of hope or expectancy. However, counselors and group leaders are in a unique position to ignite hope in students who do not yet see in themselves the strengths that others can see in them. When we hold firmly to the expectation that a student can and will step into a more satisfying life, that belief is contagious. When we see the best in students, they can see it in themselves. What we focus on expands.

Model or Theoretical Orientation

The psychological model accounts for 15 percent of change. Of all the findings in the research on change in counseling, the small contribution of the model of therapy and the related techniques is perhaps the most surprising. While the model or theoretical orientation is a relatively small contributor to change, the model directly impacts the way the practitioner harnesses the participant and relationship factors. Furthermore, a model that inherently promotes hope or expectancy supports the creation of meaningful change in participants. Therefore, it is essential that the group leader chooses a model or theoretical orientation that amplifies the other three factors, fits well within a school setting, and is a good match for both student expectations and for the group leader's personal style.

A Fifth Change Agent: The Group

The four factors noted above are based on individual counseling. Group counseling is related, but it presents some additional possibilities for change. The group itself is a source of influence and change. The interactions and feedback provided by the group can be quite compelling to its members. There exists less documented research on group counseling than comparable work with individuals, but it is likely that research will ultimately validate that the group is a significant contributor to change—maybe even the most significant contributor. Until research clarifies the factors effecting change in groups, a prudent course of action is to do all we can to maximize the known factors from research on individual counseling and to make counseling groups a safe, organized, and productive situation for students.

THE IMPORTANCE OF A THEORETICAL MODEL

While theoretical orientation accounts for only 15 percent of change, it is a vital percentage because it has strong potential for amplifying the other known factors for creating change; it is also the factor over which we have the most control. As school practitioners, it is possible to plan activities without thinking about the underlying theory that supports them. In the extensive literature on counseling groups, there is a ready supply of group activities but very few of them are based on a theoretical orientation. Most curricula are based on topics such as divorce, friendship, or bullying. By combining print material and online resources, practitioners can develop a hefty personal library for groups. This library of activities can then be used as a base for planning a group when the principal approaches us and says, for example, that the fifth-grade girls are not getting along.

There is a danger in this piecemeal approach. An assortment of group activities, even if thematically connected, does not necessarily make a good group plan. Picking activities without a common theory as a base can make for a fragmented experience for students. A foundation for our choices is important; this often means modifying activities to fit within our theoretical model or orientation. Some authors have developed material using a theoretical orientation (e.g., Vernon, 2006), but most group activity collections lack this unifying force.

Running a counseling group without a theoretical orientation as a foundation is akin to an artist incorporating a variety of painting styles in the same painting; combining elements of classicism, baroque, cubism, impressionism, romanticism, and surrealism is untenable. Each of these schools of thought is unique, with important distinguishing characteristics. While separate works of art from all these schools of thought make an interesting collection in a museum, a combination of these schools in one painting is likely to create a fractured visual experience. The same is true for group counseling. When the counseling groups we lead are grounded in a theoretical orientation that is appropriate for the group needs and the setting, we are providing students with an integrated experience. When the activities we choose and the discussions we promote are consistent with that orientation, we are in an excellent position to effect change.

Approaching Change Strategically

Sometimes change happens serendipitously. We have all had that experience. One day we simply let go of an old habit that we did not want in the first place. Psychologist Martin Seligman (Seligman & Czikszentmihalyi, 2000) tells a great story about his five-year-old daughter who reminded him that she had decided to give up whining and then asked him to change . . . to stop being so grouchy! It turned his life around. His changes in thinking and behavior spawned the movement now called positive psychology. Serendipity is a wonderful thing. Without diminishing the potential for this lively force in all our lives, it is also true that we can approach change strategically. That is what we do when we plan a group counseling curriculum that is solidly anchored in a theoretical orientation.

The leader's theoretical orientation or theory of change underscores what she or he believes about how change occurs. Students are referred for group counseling because they, or someone else, believe something needs to change. This is an essential point. Change is the goal. The goal of all groups, no matter what the orientation, is to create situations and experiences that foster change. A successful group experience can be measured by the students' changes in thinking and behavior subsequent to the group experience.

How a Theoretical Orientation Directly Affects Students

Our theoretical orientation becomes the framework around which we understand a student and the group. It also influences which behaviors and student statements we ignore and which ones we amplify in the group exchanges. A theory of change provides a certain continuity of experience for the students and a road map for the leader. Without this guiding orientation, it is easy to lose our bearing as leaders; it is like sailing without a rudder. Without a theoretical orientation, we are like Dixie cups in the ocean.

If Theoretical Models Are So Important, Why Aren't They More Widely Used?

Given the importance of a theory of change, it is unfortunate that in a recent survey of 802 school counselors (Steen, Bauman, & Smith, 2007), the vast majority of counselors did not base their counseling groups on a theoretical orientation. In terms of strategy or technique, the least used group practice was establishing client goals. Without an orientation as a rudder or a goal as a destination, group counseling seems doomed to flounder.

We can only speculate about the reasons that most counseling groups are either atheoretical or only loosely based on theory. Potential reasons include insufficient training, lack of research on effective practices, and an undervaluing of the importance of a model by practitioners. Counselors may unwittingly use the approach that is most comfortable without attending to approaches supported by research. Whatever the cause, the outcome for students appears to be that they are more routinely involved in group counseling that is less likely to produce change in an effective manner.

Is the Problem Really Insufficient Time?

It has been argued by several researchers that time is the main impediment to offering counseling groups. There is no doubt that this is an issue. It is also the case that offering a counseling group that is ill conceived will likely be unproductive and unlikely to lead to change in students. For the practitioner, it may be easier to avoid repeating a negative experience: If nothing changed, why do it again?

A more thoughtful approach would be to dig in and figure out what did work, what did not work, and eliminate the problem. This kind of assessment is easier to make when there is a framework or model as a reference point. It is easier to see why a specific activity or discussion in a group was poorly received when we consider it within the context of our model. But in the whirling blur that often is the school environment, it takes determination to be a reflective group leader. A theoretical orientation is an excellent starting point.

CHOOSING A FOUNDATION: AN EXPLORATION OF MODELS

There are many models to choose from when considering a theoretical orientation for group counseling. As noted earlier, there is no single right model, but some may be a better fit than others for the school environment. For this reason, practitioners may consider using one model as a first choice and switching to another when it becomes clear that the needs of the group dictate a change in approach.

Psychodynamic

Most "psychotherapists" on television or in the movies are portrayed getting clients to talk about their feelings. Movies such as *What About Bob?, Good Will Hunting,* or *The Sixth Sense* or the TV series *The Sopranos* fall into this category. This is what the general public and novice graduate students expect from a counselor. In this model, problems are caused by unconscious, internal conflicts. It is assumed that talking about one's feelings will lead to insight. This insight will then help the person resolve the angst that brought him or her to therapy. This approach to solving problems is called a psychodynamic orientation. A leader running a group with students from this perspective would be oriented toward expression of feelings. While this orientation is used less frequently in schools today, most parents assume this is the orientation used by practitioners when asked to give permission for group counseling. We can correct this impression by writing clear letters of permission to parents. This is discussed in detail in Chapter 6.

Cognitive-Behavioral

A leader who believes that change is most likely to occur when students change their irrational thoughts and the related negative feelings (as well as their behaviors) is likely working from a cognitive-behavioral orientation. It is assumed that the way we think affects the way we feel. Faulty thinking leads to negative emotions, and problem behavior may be the result. The goal of treatment is to help people with the way they think so they can change the way they act. This approach tends to be action-oriented, problem-solving, and focused on present thinking and behavior.

In a group setting, activities and discussions are consistent with this model or approach to change. For example, Vernon (2006) recommends an activity with fifth and sixth graders designed to help them recognize that their feelings change when their thoughts change. Scenarios are presented and students individually respond by writing their feelings and thoughts. In one situation, students are asked to imagine, "You have just been selected for the All Stars Baseball Team. The game begins in a few minutes" (p. 223). Individual differences become apparent as members share their reactions to the same situation. Some students may find this to be a thrilling prospect, while others may find it terrifying. Differences in feelings lead to differences in thinking. Some students may think "This is the best day of my life," while others may think it is one of the worst. The discussion that follows focuses on questions such as, *Have you ever changed your feelings because you changed your thoughts?* This model can be used effectively in schools.

Behavioral

This model is based on the principles of basic learning and behavior modification. The goal is to shape observable maladaptive behavior and substitute new positive responses based on consequences, reinforcement, extinction, and negative reinforcement. Change occurs as the practitioner reinforces acceptable behaviors and takes active steps to suppress undesirable behaviors. Desirable behaviors can also be modeled. This orientation is particularly helpful when the primary goals for group counseling are behaviorally oriented, such as helping students with impulse control issues.

Solution Focused

From a solution-focused perspective, the goal is to help students by constructing solutions rather than dwelling on problems. The key assumption is that problems do not happen all the time; there are times when the problem does not exist or is less intense. Therefore, elements of the solution already exist. The therapeutic task is to shift the focus away from the problem and highlight instead the exceptions to the problem. Students are encouraged to do more of what is already working in their lives and build on small successes. This is the essence of a strength-based model of counseling where the students' strengths and resources become pivotal. Success breeds success.

Solution-focused brief counseling is future focused and goal oriented. The student's goals are framed in positive terms so that what becomes clear is what the student does want, rather than what the student does not want. A comment from the famous ice hockey player Wayne Gretsky captures this future orientation: "I skate to where the puck is going, not to where it's been." This model will be discussed in detail in the following chapter. A review of the research to date (Gingerich & Eisengart, 2000) suggests that solution-focused brief counseling is an effective model for use in schools.

Which Model?

The decision on which theoretical model to use as a basis for our counseling groups is dependent on several factors: the goals and theme of the group, the developmental needs of the members, the setting, and the leader's training and experience. The list of models provided here is not exhaustive; the point is that there are choices to be made, and these choices affect student outcomes. Our objective as thoughtful group leaders is to make an informed choice about the model we use when leading counseling groups.

The theoretical orientation we choose should be a good match for the issues of the group. For example, a group of third-grade boys with ADHD is probably a better match for a behavioral or cognitive-behavioral approach than a psychodynamic approach. In addition, the orientation we work from informs our planning and the way we modify an activity to be consistent with that model of change. If we are working from a psychodynamic orientation, we might end an activity by talking about how the activity made students feel—something we are much less likely to do from a solution-focused approach.

The model we use provides guidance at difficult decision points when leading a group. For example, imagine a leader mired in conversations with fifth-grade girls that are problem saturated and circular (lots of complaining about who did what to whom). From a solution-focused perspective, once the girls feel heard, these endless complaints are probably not useful. Working from this model, the leader would shift the conversation away from the problem-dominated discourse and ask instead about times when the problems do not exist.

Why Not Simply Use the Best Parts of Each Model?

Can you blend models? Take the best parts of each? The answer to this is both yes and no. There are aspects of some models that make good sense no matter what model the practitioner is using. For example, the focus on student strengths and resources might work well regardless of the model. However, the assumptions about how change occurs are quite different—and in some ways contradictory—in each of the models briefly described. In a solution-focused group, talking about feelings may be appropriate for developing group cohesion and establishing commonality, but it is not assumed that change occurs as a result of the conversation. The conversation serves a useful purpose, but it is not an end point. In contrast, for a psychodynamic leader who is less oriented toward goals and more focused on process, the conversation about feelings might be an end point without ever arriving at a concrete solution or idea about what to do next.

A Single Perfect Theoretical Model Doesn't Exist

The essential question to ask ourselves is not which model is best, but rather which model is best for this specific situation. Recent research on various theoretical models over a forty year span indicates that there is no one perfect theoretical model (Asay & Lambert, 1999). No single approach has proven to be more effective than others. Therapists foster change by maximizing relationships, developing hope and expectancy, and building on client strengths. The model or theoretical orientation the therapist chooses to promote change accounts for only 15 percent of effective change. After years of scholarly competition about which model is best, it turns out that everyone wins. It is the commonalities rather than the differences in the various theoretical orientations that are significant. Extending this research to group counseling suggests that there are choices to be made.

Why Solution-Focused Principles Are a Great Match for School Groups

Solution-focused brief counseling is not the only way to work effectively with students to produce change, but it is a practical and intuitively sensible approach for working with students in a school setting. In an era of accountability, it is a model with an explicit focus on goals and change. In this way, it is a school-friendly app-roach. It is also a model that teachers, administrators, and parents can readily understand. When it comes to granting permission for group counseling, parents are more amenable when there is a stated goal that makes intuitive sense. Many authors have applied the solution-focused model to individual counseling (e.g., Murphy, 2008; Sklare, 2005), but less has been written about applying solution-focused ideas to school counseling groups. The next chapter is devoted to what it looks like when school counseling groups are based on the principles and assumptions of solution-focused brief counseling.

PRACTITIONER TRAINING

As practitioners, we work with students because we want to help, to contribute. But without the training to provide that help, we can become well-intentioned do-gooders with a low probability of being able to actually make a difference.

When courses in group counseling are offered in graduate schools, it is common for the instructor to have the class become a "group" and the instructor to become a group leader. In these situa-tions, the class becomes a quasi group-therapy situation. Regardless of the merits or disadvantages of this approach to training, one thing is certain: Graduate students do *not* learn how to run groups in ele-mentary and secondary schools by talking about their fear of failure or even their successes with classmates. Thus, it is not surprising that many educators enter the school environment unprepared to organize and run groups.

The purpose of this book is to give the practitioner whose training was thin and the graduate student who is new to the field an equal opportunity to learn how to lead successful school counseling groups. We all want to make a difference. This book will help you do just that.

SUMMARY

As mental health practitioners working in schools, we have a unique opportunity to support students by offering group counseling. Advances in our field mean we now know a great deal more about what creates change: client factors, relationship factors, hope, and the model or theoretical orientation. We can use this information to our advantage. Our informed choices may take us on a journey from the way we have always done it into unfamiliar territory. The challenges inherent in learning something new will be rewarded by seeing the difference we can make.

Momentum in the field has shifted from a spotlight on the *process* to a focus on the *outcome*. The advent of data-based decision making and research-based programs has helped shift the focus to outcome. What we do in our student contact is important, but whether it actually produces results is equally so. Researchers have a heightened interest in change and how to create it. The model of change used by the practitioner in group counseling becomes the platform for creating and supporting changes in the lives of our students. There is no one best model or theoretical orientation, but some models of counseling may be a better fit in a school environment. Given the importance of the model of change, it merits careful consideration.

CHAPTER TWO

Solution-Focused Counseling

A Primer

Solution-focused brief counseling (SFBC) was a radical idea in the 1980s when the model was new. It was revolutionary to consider that conversations about *solutions,* not conversations about *problems,* would lead to change in clients. This radical idea was initially dismissed by some who saw the model as simplistic and unlikely to lead to lasting change. However, the innovation of the early pioneers was quickly matched by enthusiasm from practitioners eager for results and from the insurance industry, which saw this model as a way to provide briefer treatment. Beginning in 1982, The Milwaukee Family Therapy Institute, under the direction of Steve deShazer and Insoo Kim Berg, became a magnet for like-minded or curious practitioners. A publication burst popularized SFBC even further in the years that followed, beginning with the work of Steve deShazer (1985, 1988).

Counseling from a solution-focused perspective fits under the more inclusive heading of strength-based approaches in mental health. Solution-focused brief counseling, and strength-based approaches in general, move away from an archeological dig into the participant's past and toward identifying and building on strengths. This is a distinct shift from past practices. In these models, the focus is on the participant's strengths, not on the deficits. The idea is simple and compelling: We can get more change by focusing on what does work rather than on what does not. These models have an easy appeal to both practitioners and the general public.

Since its inception, much has been written on solution-focused counseling for individual students in schools, but little has been written on applying solution-focused ideas to school groups. The distinction between a more general group and a solution-focused group is an important one. The typical group counseling approach focuses on getting students to talk about their issues, process what's happening, and share their feelings. In contrast, a counseling group with a strength-based approach focuses on goals, what the student wants to do differently, and personal strengths. The solution-focused model is consistent with current trends in education: It emphasizes data-based decision making, positive behavior change, and measurable outcomes. It is a brief model that works particularly well in schools.

SFBC is a way to orient a counseling group. It is also a way to orient a school (see Metcalf, 2008). Let's look at the assumptions and principles of solution-focused thinking and apply the ideas to the school as a system and to individuals before applying these ideas to counseling groups. It will be easier to examine solution-focused ideas within this familiar school context before expanding to small counseling groups.

THE SCHOOL AS A SYSTEM

While SFBC has become mainstream for mental health practitioners, it remains somewhat novel to most educators. For the staff at large, the ideas behind SFBC practices are easy to digest and implement as long as everything is going relatively well at the school. Who could argue against noticing student strengths or promoting resiliency by developing alternative programs that let all students experience success outside the classroom? But when trouble is brewing—for example, when students are referred to the office for behavior problems—the inclination is to retreat to the "default model" (or standard way of operating) at the school. When the predominant operating mode is the default model, which is generally more punitive, what we hear in the staff room are comments such as "He has to take responsibility for his actions" or "We need to discuss the consequences for that behavior." More creative energy seems to go into the consequences than into the preferred behavior. Even though we know that we are more likely to change behavior with positive strategies than with negative ones, we somehow drift back into consequences without fully investigating the possibility of focusing on what is already working for the student.

To be clear, there is nothing wrong with consequences. And there is certainly nothing wrong with wanting a student to take responsibility for his or her actions. But we should also be clear that change is less likely to result from these interactions alone. If we keep our eye on the ultimate goal of improved behavior, from a solution-focused perspective, the consequences must be balanced with other strategies that increase the possibility that the maladaptive behavior will be decreased. Students need to have something to work *toward* and a reason to work toward it. Building on success and noticing what is working for the student is the foundation for the desired change.

Emily and Her Homework

What does the default model look like when we are functioning as a member of the school student study team? This group of school professionals and parents meets to discuss ways to help students who are struggling to be more successful. Let's imagine that Emily, a fourth grader with behavior problems, is being discussed. She is a likable student who gets along well with peers and adults, and she does well in school. She has, however, been refusing to do her home-work, much to the irritation of her teacher and her parents. At first, her parents did not notice this homework problem; they learned about it at a parent-teacher conference a month after it began. Since that time, several consequences have been initiated. If Emily does not turn in her homework at the appointed time, she must stay in dur-ing recess that day until she is finished. If she does not finish during recess, she also misses her free time at lunch. The conversation in which these consequences were made and agreed to by the teacher, parents, and other school staff reflects a sincere attempt to get Emily to take responsibility for her actions.

Does this sound familiar? This is what I am referring to as the default model. It is the typical school response—a disciplinary approach that is based on consequences. Unless some positive aspects are added to this plan, this approach has the potential for some unwanted side effects. From a solution-focused perspective, the plan lacks balance. It is missing a focus on what Emily needs to move *toward*: the desired behavior.

Emily, like most fourth graders, loves recess. Some kids come to school "to eat their lunch," but Emily comes to school for the basketball and her friends. This previously happy young girl becomes distressed when facing a day without recess. You would think this would be enough to inspire her to get her homework done, but somehow that does not happen. Instead, she gets sullen and falls further behind. She is unable to concentrate during recess to finish her homework, inclined instead to look out the window to see what she is missing. The more she gets behind, the more recess she misses and the more sullen she becomes. This formerly happy student is becoming a behavior problem now as well. She is grumpy with the teacher, who begins to see her as "rude" and impatient with her friends, who do not understand why she does not join them outside. She is creating a whole new reputation for herself, and she is stigmatized at multiple levels. She was one of the "good" kids, but now she is one of the kids asked to leave the school assembly because she is not cooperating. It gets worse.

The school's student study team meets again to discuss what to do with Emily. Apparently the consequences are not working, and she is certainly not taking responsibility for her actions. The most typical response is to do more of the same. The next series of consequences is more severe: less recess and no playing outside at home after school until she is caught up on her homework. We take these kinds of actions trying to be helpful. But when we do more of what is already not working (i.e., restricting her play time), we are breaking one of the cardinal rules of a solution-focused approach: *If what you are doing isn't working, try something different.* There are alternatives to this dreary scenario.

How Could We Increase the Odds of Being Successful With Emily?

Rewind the tape to the beginning of this situation with Emily. We have a fourth grader who has stopped doing her homework. We can decide to approach this from a counseling perspective prior to a disciplining approach. We have many choices, and the actions we take are based on the model of change we use. A response to Emily based on the four models of change discussed in Chapter 1 is presented just to give a sense of the differences in the approaches. From a psychodynamic perspective, we might ask Emily how she feels about her homework and how she feels about missing recess. From a cognitive-behavioral approach, we might ask Emily what she thinks about her homework and help her sort out any faulty ideas. From a behavioral perspective, we might develop a reinforcement system that rewards even small attempts to produce some homework, gradually expecting and rewarding more positive behavior.

Any of these approaches might work effectively, depending on the delivery and the next steps. It is noteworthy that the default model discussed above, which is oriented toward discipline, might also work well with some students. The default model has a long history in education. It is usually seen as the commonsense approach and is readily understood by educators and parents. The problem is that it does not always work, especially with students who are more troubled. The students who are referred to the mental health practitioners in the schools are not usually easy cases. Often, the default model has already been tried with little to no success. Our input is sought when the obvious strategies do not work.

Thinking about Emily from a solution-focused perspective, we might begin by noticing that for the three previous years, Emily had faithfully done her homework and handed it in with pride. If we want to build on success, then her homework history is the obvious starting point. If she was doing her homework all along, how was she doing it? We can investigate what she was doing successfully in order to return to the previous happy state. We can talk with Emily, approaching her as a student with an excellent homework history, and ask her how she was able to get her homework done all those years. These conversations show what it means to build on success. And since Emily is the expert on her problem, we can ask her what it would take to support her in getting her homework done efficiently so that she would not have to miss any recess.

During this conversation with Emily, we might discover that her aging grandfather, who has Alzheimer's disease, moved into her home at the same time that Emily stopped doing her homework. We might learn that she is both worried about him and a little frightened. It is easy to see that this development could upset her normal approach to homework. Counselors working from other orientations might quietly utter "Aha!" and delve into Emily's feelings about her grandfather or any irrational thoughts she might have concerning him. Their idea is that change will occur when Emily understands and has insight about her thoughts and feelings.

In contrast, from a solution-focused approach, Emily's thoughts and feelings about her grandfather are important and attended to, but are *not* seen as the basis for change. A soothing and supportive conversation with Emily builds the relationship between the student and practitioner; as explored in the previous chapter, the relationship between student and practitioner is one of the most important ingredients for change. It might not, however, help Emily figure out what to do next. She needs help sorting out what steps to take to make her life work more smoothly. From a solution-focused perspective, it is important to ask Emily questions that rely on her expertise. The following are sample questions from a conversation with Emily:

- *How have you dealt with this change in your family?*
- *How have you managed to get as much homework done as you have under the circumstances?*
- *What will it take to get more homework done under the circumstances?*

Conversations that allow her to demonstrate her strengths and resourcefulness (i.e., *"Sometimes I did my homework in the backyard or at a friend's house"*) allow us to take that information and build on it. The task for us is to help construct a world with her where she can do more of what is already working. Instead of asking "Why didn't you do you homework?" we are asking *"How have you managed as well as you have?"* The first question is from the default model, and the second question is solution focused.

Advocacy Within the School System

It takes effort to work against the current at our schools and promote other ways of looking at student problems. What this means for us as practitioners is that we will most likely need to function as an advocate for new ways of approaching problems. Our influence campaign can be a quiet one. It requires consistency, a clear understanding of our purpose, and knowledge that we can gradually share with others. Influencing a system can be a slow process. But the questions we ask can turn around a meeting about a student who is careening toward a dead end. Imagine what might have happened if we had asked the group at that first meeting on Emily the following question: *So how has Emily managed to be so successful with homework in the past?* This nonantagonistic question shifts the focus 180 degrees. Once this new conversation is launched, we have the opportunity to surreptitiously influence the groupthink. There is so much more to work with when the focus is on what's working.

THE ASSUMPTIONS OF SOLUTION-FOCUSED BRIEF COUNSELING

The assumptions of solution-focused brief counseling take on a slightly different complexion depending on the author. Every solution-focused author has a different emphasis or way of organizing the information. Despite variability of focus among writers, there is general agreement on the eight assumptions that are listed here and discussed below.

1. All students have resources and strengths, even if they are not yet obvious to us or to the student.

2. If what you are doing is working, do more of it. If what you are doing isn't working, at least try something different.

3. Problems are not constant. There are times when the problem either does not exist or is less frequent.

4. Big problems do not necessarily require complex solutions.

5. Changes in one area will affect other areas.

6. Even if temporarily confused or uncertain, the student is the expert on the problem.

7. The solution may not necessarily be directly related to the problem. The solution can be found at the intersection of the future focus, the student's strengths and resourcefulness, and the counselor's respectful curiosity.

8. Change is inevitable.

The counselor's ability to internalize these beliefs is a critical part of working from a solution-focused perspective. SFBC is based on a specific way of viewing people. The practitioners who are successful with this model are those who believe these assumptions about people and life circumstances. As you review these assumptions, do so with an eye toward whether the assumption is already consistent with your belief system or whether you need to put energy into shifting your current beliefs. If you have not yet considered the merits of one or more of these assumptions, you have an opportunity to stretch your thinking.

Assumption 1

All students have resources and strengths, even if they are not yet obvious to us or to the student.

What this means for us as practitioners is that we see the best in students, even when their best is well hidden. This is not a blindly optimistic approach—we do see the issues. Taking this position does not mean that we condone unacceptable behavior. It does mean that we are undeterred in our ability to see the strengths in a student who also exhibits appalling behavior. As educators, we routinely advise parents to separate the behavior from the child and deal with the behavior without assuming that their child *is* the bad behavior; we do the same in solution-focused counseling. The student is not the problem; the problem is the problem. This is no small distinction. When we see the student as the problem, he or she becomes an irritant. We have less leverage to influence change when students conclude that we see them as unlikable; we are easy to write off when we cannot see their strengths.

To work under the influence of this assumption, we have to believe in our hearts that students have the strengths and resources necessary to solve their problems. Our job is to ask good questions and help students access those strengths. Imagine how surprised a gang leader will be when we ask, *"How is it that others in your group have come to see you as a leader? How have you managed to keep their respect? They have choices about leadership, so how did they pick you?"* The predictable bravado responses about how the group is scared of the gang leader are a way to scare us off; at this point, we look like all the other previous "helpers." The bravado is a way to derail us, but with relentless and patient questions, even the committed gang leader can be persuaded to talk about his or her leadership skills. We can highlight the qualities in the gang leader that might work best for success at school. Once we are engaged in a conversation about strengths, we are on the way to building the relationship we need to influence change. It all starts with seeing the best in students, even when they present with extremely "gnarly" behavior!

The assumption that every student has strengths and resources can be difficult for practitioners new to solution-focused thinking. It often draws a response of "OK, but what about the kid who lies, cheats, and steals from everyone including his grandmother? How can we see any strengths in this kid?" When we let these kinds of questions creep into our thoughts, we are seeing the glass as half empty. We are missing the chance to see students as resourceful. The more interesting thought is, *"I wonder what was different about the times he could have lied and didn't. I wonder who is on the short list of folks he would never cheat."* We need to start with students where they are by asking questions that invite them to reveal their strengths, not their warts.

Let's go back to Emily. Learning that she had been successful with homework in the past was a stroke of good fortune; this was the obvious starting point. But what if she did not have a good homework history? Where do we go then? Look for strengths anywhere. Maybe Emily is a dedicated older sibling, or maybe she is kind to the little boy down the street who has few friends. Maybe Emily likes to draw and generously shares her pictures with others. Any of these strengths that are seemingly unrelated to homework can be woven back into the current dilemma. It takes patience to spend time with a younger neighbor, and she has likely taught him many new things. It may be worth asking how she learned to be patient in this way, who was the best teacher for her, and how she handles it when she runs out of patience. Students love to talk about their strengths. Don't we all? The carryover question might be to ask how patience is helpful to her when she has homework to do and how patience could be more helpful. As the expert on patience, we might also inquire about any advice she could give her young neighbor about doing homework just in case he runs into any difficulty. As she positively coaches him, she is coaching herself.

Logarithmic Gains for a Group

The possibilities for promoting change by seeing strengths and resources reaches logarithmic proportions when applied to group counseling. When we see the best in others, they can see it in themselves and in one another in the group. There are many ways that a leader can become aware that a group has become oriented toward strengths and resources. Students might, for example, spontaneously offer compliments and encouragement to each other. This is particularly valuable when the compliment is about a goal not yet attained. Sometimes they offer advice that the leader could never share, but we thank our good fortune that the comments were made. There are other ways students demonstrate an esprit de corps. Sometimes group members will want to create a name for the group or extend the number of meetings. At the secondary level, there is sometimes a move to meet for lunch or have a pizza party. The positive momentum that develops over time contributes to a safe environment that permits authentic conversations; from within this safe setting, students can take a risk with change.

Assumption 2

If what you are doing is working, do more of it. If what you are doing isn't working, at least try something different.

It is important to remember to do more of what is already working or has worked in the past. For example, imagine a parent consulting a therapist about a parenting issue that occurs episodically. Every few years, the son goes through an annoying cycle of rude behavior. A crucial question to ask at this point is, *"What did you do the last time that happened?"* And then, *"Did it work?"* Since the problem went away, the odds are that the strategy worked in the past, and the family just needs to remember to do it again. If what you did worked, do it again.

If what you are doing is not working, at least try something different. This assumption sounds so obvious that it is almost comical. "Of course!" you say. "Why would I repeat something that was a failure?" Ironically, we do. As educators in the example with Emily, we lengthened her playground restriction when it was unsuccessful. It did not work, and yet we unwittingly did more of it.

Here is an example from everyday life. Have you ever been in a restaurant where you did not speak the local language and the people in the restaurant did not speak English? Think of yourself wanting a tomato. Most of us would ask for something we want by saying it slowly in our native language and accompanying it with hand gestures, hoping that the English word and the foreign word are close cousins. When that is unsuccessful, what do most of us do? We repeat the same slow and deliberate words and hand gestures, but this time we say it louder and use more dramatic gestures. Our approach did not work the first time, and yet we are inclined to repeat it. Puzzling, isn't it? Most of us would eventually point or make a sketch on a napkin, but usually we get stuck in our funny little repetition before we realize we need to try something different.

Doing Something Different in a Group

In counseling groups, if reminding Rachael, a fifth grader, to take turns (so she'll stop interrupting!) is not successful, then continuing to remind her is probably useless and will likely lead to frustration. We need a different idea. Maybe it's time to introduce a "talking stick," a Native American tradition where only the person holding the stick can talk and all others must listen. In counseling groups, the nature of the group situation lends itself to trying new things; when something we have done in the past needs to be changed, students are usually preoccupied enough with each other and the group in general that there is an almost built-in capacity to roll with the changes we initiate.

It is ironic that as we coach students to change, we often stumble in this area ourselves. We have a hard time switching gears. There seems to be a hardwired tendency to repeat what is not working, a tendency we can teach ourselves to overcome. Perhaps we are working against modeling in our own lives, repeating the choices made by our parents and teachers. In any case, working from a solution-focused perspective invites us to be more elastic, to entertain possibilities. The practice is as good for us as it is for the students.

Assumption 3

Problems are not constant. There are times when the problem either does not exist or is less frequent.

By the time we see parents who are frustrated with a son or daughter, they may have slipped into overgeneralizing as a way of expressing their distress. Overgeneralizing shows up in the use of key words like "he always . . . (insert unwanted behavior)," or "she never . . . (insert desired behavior)." The discouraged parent can get mired in this type of all-or-nothing thinking. This makes the problem seem intractable and larger than it needs to be.

As educators, we are prone to the same distortions in our thinking. In a staff room, when teachers are disheartened and feel unprepared to meet the challenges they face, we hear the same overgeneralizing. The antidote from a solution-focused perspective is to search for exceptions to the problem, times when the problem does not exist. Once the teacher or parent feels we have heard and understood his or her situation, our goal is to loosen the grip of the problem by asking questions about the nonproblematic times. The assumption is that the unwanted behavior does not happen all the time.

Margaret, a second grader, has developed some unwanted ways of coping. Margaret's parents have separated. She is an only child: She is crushed by this development and has no siblings or cousins to rely on. She is weepy in class, socially withdrawn, and hypersensitive to criticism. When this issue first arose, she received lots of support and encouragement from the teacher. It has been several months now, and Margaret has not improved. The teacher is becoming impatient with Margaret and is beginning to see her tearfulness as manipulative, as using the impending divorce as an excuse for not doing her work.

At this point, the default approach would be to ask about the problem. This seems like the normal and sensible thing to do. But from a solution-focused approach, we would take the opposite tact. In a radical shift of focus, the solution can be found in the times the problem does not exist, the times when Margaret is not weepy. The moments Margaret seems engaged like other second graders are the moments that hold the most promise for solving the problem. Despite the fact that Margaret has been described as weepy or crying *all the time,* under closer examination, it is apparent that she is tuned in during story time, loves to run errands to the office, and is a delighted whiz on the computer reading program. During these times, she is indistinguishable from the rest of the class. While all of school cannot be errands to the office, computer games, or stories, these situations hold keys to more happiness for Margaret. As super-sleuths, our job is to sort out what is going on during these nonproblem times. With the information about exceptions to the problem, we can help the teacher strategize about how to amplify her positive behavior.

Getting the Group to Talk About Exceptions

In group counseling, operating under the assumption that there are exceptions to the problem means that we take advantage of the opportunity to shift conversations away from an overfocus on the problem. Instead, we promote conversations in which the problem is less apparent, less of a burden, or not an issue at all. This takes some practice. We are sometimes relieved that students are actually talking with each other and bonding when engaged in a problem-saturated conversation. They can get revved up complaining about a common issue such as teachers who are unfair. This can be a good starting point for developing group cohesion, but from a solution-focused perspective, it is not the mechanism for creating change. When the group is able to focus on exceptions to the problem, envision a future without the problem, and set goals, the potential for real change emerges. Our goal is to get students to talk about teachers they like and how these teachers influence their work and behavior. This conversation about exceptions is the stepping stone to real change.

The following assumptions—4, 5, and 6—are closely related and will be jointly applied to group counseling following the discussion of Assumption 6.

Assumption 4

Big problems do not necessarily require complex solutions.

The life circumstances of some students are so overwhelming that it is hard to imagine how they survive at all. Then we meet a student or hear about a family with even greater challenges. As mental health practitioners in the school, the potential for feeling like we are in quicksand is a risk we must manage attentively. Fortunately, big problems do not necessarily call for remarkable solutions. This assumption may come as a relief. This is a model in which simpler may be better and creativity is valued.

Sometimes the shift that makes all the difference is a small one. In a conversation with a group of graduate students, one woman discussed how overwhelmed she felt by the mounting pressure in her internship, the sheer volume of her academic work, the needs of her two children, and her longing to have more time with her husband. As she talked about it, she seemed to sink deeper into a mild despair. It was not until someone asked her what was different on the days that were a little better that her spirits lifted. Her response was amazingly simple. She said she felt better on the days she made her bed in the morning. Something about having the bed made helped her feel more in control of the day. When she felt more in control of the day, the gnawing feeling of drowning in her work was not present. It was a striking conversation, both for the simplicity and for the power inherent in her strategy. Making her bed was certainly not going to make all the issues disappear like a cloud of talcum powder, but believing she had more control over her day was a momentous start.

Assumption 5

Changes in one area will affect other areas.

We see this all the time. Our shy neighbor starts an exercise program, begins to get in shape and lose weight. He carries himself more confidently. Somehow he does not seem so shy anymore. He waves when he drives by and sometimes says hello. Now he talks to neighbors who greet him when he is out mowing the lawn, something he religiously avoided in the past. All these changes followed a New Year's resolution to start exercising; changes in one area have a ripple effect on other areas. Our goal is to get that first stone in the water so the ripple can begin.

Assumption 6

Even if temporarily confused or uncertain, the student is the expert on the problem.

For experienced practitioners contemplating a shift from more traditional models (where the practitioner is the expert) to a solution-focused approach, this assumption can be difficult to accept. If we have been in the field for a while, we are accustomed to being asked for advice and making recommendations. We have years of training, degrees, and credentials. We are seen by parents, staff, and the local pediatrician as mental health experts at the school site. With all our credibility, how is it that the problem student just became the expert?

One way of thinking about it is to review how often students with a problem have listened carefully to our sage advice and then sprung from the chair saying *"What a good idea. That's exactly what I'm going to do!"* Ever? Isn't that what we are expecting when we give advice? Maybe we imagine that our advice will percolate and lead to change over time. The expectation is that students will see the merits of our position and make good choices accordingly.

In most counseling models, the therapist is seen as the expert. Based on expert knowledge of psychology, the counselor or therapist directs the conversation and has goals for the client. The counselor is the one who judges whether the counseling was successful. Some models, such as cognitive-behavioral therapy, are not as vulnerable to the advice-giving trap—but with the exception of the strength-based models (e.g., narrative therapy), most models see the therapist as the expert. In solution-focused brief counseling, the client is the expert. So what does it mean to say the client is the expert? Practically speaking, it means we resign from the advice-giving department.

From a solution-focused perspective, the client knows more about the problem than we do. Ladonna, who is fourteen years old, may not yet know how to get out of the proverbial box in which she finds herself. The key words here are *not yet.* But she does know a lot about rumbling around in there. She is beginning to find the box cramped and uncomfortable. From a solution-focused perspective, we are less interested in *how* she got in there and more interested in helping her plot her escape. Our job is to ask questions that help her create a plan. From a position of respectful curiosity, we can ask about times when she has lifted the lid just a little. How did she do it? She may tell us why the lid slammed down again and how awful it was when that happened. Careful and responsive listening is important at this juncture. Once she feels we understand her, we can promote a conversation that explores her strengths. A more useful conversation is to wonder with her how she got up the nerve to lift the lid in the first place. If she did it once, she can do it again. We might ask her who knew she had it in her to make a move, who believed in her. How has this helped her believe in herself? She may tell us her doubts about ever getting out, and when she does we listen *loudly,* as this conversation helps to strengthen the bond between the counselor and the student. Take note: Our empathetic response is really important, but it may not be enough to help her figure out what to do next. From a solution-focused perspective, this is not enough to create change. Our task is to help her discover what she needs to *do.*

This conversation could be on a wide variety of topics. Replace the box with a bad reputation. Ladonna is the one who is the expert on having a bad reputation; since we believe students are resourceful, she is the one who knows how to change it. Our stance of respectful curiosity acknowledges her expertise and lends support as we strategize with her about how to develop a better reputation.

When we see the client as the expert, there is a reduced burden on the counselor to have all the answers. Clearly the counselor has expertise, but rather than using that expertise to tell the students what to do, we use it to help the students formulate their own goals and strategize with them about how to reach those goals.

Applying Several Assumptions to Group Counseling

Big problems do not necessarily require complex solutions.

Changes in one area will affect other areas.

Even if temporarily confused or uncertain, the client is the expert on the problem.

Applying the last three assumptions to group counseling demonstrates the power of simplicity. Imagine a group of ethnically diverse middle school boys and girls who all live in foster care. The conversation is about how to make friends given the frequency of being moved to new homes and different schools. One student mentions the embarrassment he feels about having peers know he lives in a foster home. Another mentions the lack of privacy as she has to share a room with someone she does not know well; she wants privacy more than friends. All agree that it is difficult to handle school when they transfer midyear; nearly all the students are behind in school. Some students miss their family of origin, but others are relieved to be out of that home. This is a poignant conversation for most leaders, and the good news is they are all talking.

Friendship is a difficult issue for students who live in foster care. The leader introduces the idea of setting personal goals related to friendship to the group. The first pass at establishing goals is ignored by the group, who seem to be enjoying sharing their experiences and comparing notes. After a brief time, the leader makes another attempt at goal setting but this time offers more acknowledgment of all they have been through. This softened approach facilitates an ability to make a shift. The leader asks, *What is going on in your life now that you would like to have continue?* Several participants respond with a degree of goofiness: lunch, sitting behind the cute guy in algebra, not having any homework in P.E. The leader asks, *What's one small thing that would make you feel more comfortable with people at school?* One of the girls, Amy, says she would like to get to know the girl she sits next to in English. Her comment shifts the group into a more serious conversation. What she wants is a small thing: to see about a friendship with the girl she sees every school day. She lives in a world of social flux, where meaningful relationships are ended in a flash when a teen is abruptly moved to a new school. Some students in foster care give up on making friends altogether. But Amy is willing to risk trying to connect with a peer. It's admirable, really. Although one could easily say that Amy has multiple challenges in her life, her goal is simple. *Big problems do not necessarily require complex solutions.*

At this point, the leader and the members are in a position to help Amy strategize about how to meet her goal. While questions may be directed at Amy, all group members will benefit; when Amy talks, others inevitably try out the ideas in their own mind and may also contribute their thoughts. Several questions are possible here:

What is already happening that helps you see a friendship is possible?

What will be the first small steps you can take to get to know her?

What have you tried in the past that you thought worked well for you when making friends?

How will you know that you are on the right path?

How do you think making friends with this girl will affect your ability to make other friends?

With this last question, the conversation will expand beyond one friend to the possibility of making others. Amy may also eventually consider the group members as friends, but it is too early to ask about this possibility. As she takes steps in forming a friendship, and as she is successful, she will build confidence to do it again—a confidence she will need to fortify herself when she has to move and start the process all over again. To paraphrase Steve deShazer, with her first steps at friendship, the snowball is started down the hill. *Changes in one area will affect other areas.*

From a solution-focused perspective, Amy is the expert on what it takes for her to make social connections. She may be bewildered or stuck at the moment. She may lack confidence to take the first steps. But with thoughtful questions designed to access her personal perspective, she can access the information she needs to go forward. What she does *not* need is a leader telling her what to do. Group members can offer advice or share experiences without diminishing her expert position, but when the leader offers advice, it robs Amy of her expertise. Our ability to communicate what we believe without saying a word has a profound effect on students. They have antennae for rejection and criticism. Likewise, students know when we believe in them. When we see them as experts, they see it in themselves. *Even if temporarily confused or uncertain, the client is the expert on the problem.*

Assumption 7

The solution may not necessarily be directly related to the problem. The solution can be found at the intersection of the future focus, the student's strengths and resourcefulness, and the counselor's respectful curiosity.

Steve deShazer (1985) introduced the notion that problems are like locks and solutions are like keys. Rather than assume that every lock has a highly specific key, he saw skeleton keys as a better analogy; skeleton keys have the ability to open many different locks, like a master key in today's parlance. He was far more interested in the key than the lock; in his work he found that many specific interventions, like master keys, worked effectively with clients regardless of the issue that brought them into therapy. The *formula-first task, miracle question, exceptions to the problem,* and *scaling* are examples of skeleton keys. These interventions will be discussed in detail in the next chapter.

The key opens the lock and unleashes a solution that may not be directly related to the problem. The student's solution may be strikingly simple, such as making a bed. The essential feature is that it is the student's personal solution, whether it is directly related to the problem or not. Just as there is no one-to-one correspondence between the lock and the skeleton key, there is also no one-to-one correspondence between the problem and the solution. From this perspective, there are many ways to unlock a door.

Assumption 8

Change is inevitable.

Even when something appears static, it is changing; this is the nature of the universe. A house left unattended for a long period of time will deteriorate. A boat deserted in the harbor will attract critters and rust. A playground that is not cared for will grow weeds. Relationships left unnurtured for long periods of time will suffer. Change is inevitable.

We have a choice about whether we focus on solutions or problems. Our students have the same choices, although they may not know it yet. They *will* change. Our job is to shine a flashlight on the possibilities by asking thoughtful questions that invite active participation in the change process. There is great freedom in knowing we have choices, even when it seems that none of the choices are good ones. The goal is to make an informed choice.

CONCLUSIONS

The following story was told by Furman and Ahola (1992) and has been adapted here to demonstrate the assumptions of solution-focused approaches to problems.

A woman living in a small town found the pharmacist increasingly rude. His behavior was unfriendly and brusque. This became increasingly distressing to her. She was unable to switch pharmacies as this was the only one in town. She discussed this situation with her friend and they concluded that something needed to be done. The friend volunteered to go speak to the pharmacist, as she could see that the woman was simply too upset.

The next time the woman visited the pharmacy, she was pleasantly surprised. The pharmacist was friendly and helpful, and the exchange was quite positive. She contacted her friend to inquire about her conversation with the pharmacist. She assumed the friend had "let him have it" and she was interested in the details.

To her astonishment, she learned that her friend had not lectured the pharmacist. On the contrary, the friend told the pharmacist that the woman found him to be charming and friendly, and that he was always gracious in his interactions with her.

The actions the friend took demonstrated that she believed that the pharmacist was capable of changing and had the resources to do so. Treating the pharmacist with displeasure clearly had not worked for the woman, so the friend did something different. We can assume the problem was not constant as he was able to change his behavior rather abruptly. This was a fairly simple interaction, neither time intensive nor emotionally draining. As the pharmacist tunes in to how he interacts with the woman, it seems likely that his more cheerful style will be contagious with other customers. The woman was the expert as she discussed it with her friend, even if her friend took a different tack in approaching the pharmacist. In this case, the solution was fairly closely related to the problem, but that was not a prerequisite for a successful outcome. The friend capitalized on the fact that change is inevitable; she just carefully chose to build on the pharmacist's strengths rather than expose his weaknesses.

Don't You Wish You'd Thought of That? You Can!

In the next chapter, we will build on these assumptions by discussing specific solution-focused techniques. Then we will apply these ideas, concepts, and techniques to small group counseling.

SUMMARY

This chapter introduced solution-focused thinking as an alternative to the default model in schools, a change from business as usual. Counseling groups led from this perspective are distinctly different from traditional groups where there is more focus on feelings and on processing what's happening. In solution-focused groups, the focus is on goals, exceptions, what the student wants to do differently, and personal strengths.

The assumptions of solution-focused brief counseling inform interventions and conversations when using this model. The practitioner is encouraged to give some thought to whether these assumptions are consistent with existing personal beliefs, or have potential to be so. Successfully working from an SFBC perspective requires the practitioner to incorporate these assumptions and to convert them into practices consistent with this model. Some of the assumptions appear startling (e.g., the client is the expert) until the notion is weighed against *what works to promote change.* In this comparison, the assumptions fair well. The assumptions for solution-focused counseling tempt the practitioner to suspend some old beliefs while considering new ones. This process is revitalizing regardless of the chosen theoretical orientation of the practitioner.

CHAPTER THREE

Turning a Solution-Focused Attitude Into Practice

In the last chapter, the assumptions of solution-focused brief counseling were examined; they are the mind-set one adopts when
working from this perspective. In this chapter, the techniques and
strategies for working from this model will be discussed. As the
counselor embraces a solution-focused mind-set, the techniques and
strategies become less formulaic and more meaningful.

Before discussing the specific techniques, two words of caution
are in order. First, a collection of interesting techniques is no substitute for a therapeutic relationship. As discussed in Chapter 1, according to research, the relationship between counselor and student
accounts for 30 percent of change. This is a 30 percent we cannot do
without. An unfortunate mistake made by new and enthusiastic counselors is to whip out a clever technique without first developing the
relationship that is a critical prerequisite for therapeutic effectiveness. Students need to feel heard, understood, and appreciated before
we can charge ahead. Perhaps it is our eagerness to help students
resolve troubling issues that propels us toward shortcuts that ultimately undo our ability to be helpful. Skimping on the development
of a solid therapeutic relationship is a shortcut to nowhere.

A second word of caution is that it often seems as if the default
model is hardwired into us in some mysterious way. There is a striking disconnect between understanding this model (SFBC) and being
able to put it into practice. Counselors who are completely new to
training seem to have an easier time than counselors who have prior

training. Based on this difficulty, it is a good idea to arrange supervision or consultation when putting this model into practice. In this case, "supervision" could mean having lunch bimonthly with a colleague who has been successfully using the model. Discussing cases and problem spots can be extremely helpful.

Group consultation is another option for support when learning a new model. One school district in northern California began the school year with a presentation I gave on solution-focused counseling and followed up with monthly small-group consultation meetings. Counselors who volunteered for the group meetings were able to count their hours as continuing education since I am a licensed practitioner. The group was so popular, and such a source of strong collegial support, that it lasted for years. This is an effective way to receive consultation while learning a new model of counseling. As a fortuitous by-product, consultation in small groups also addresses many other professional needs (such as continuing education requirements) and helps meet worthwhile objectives such as reduced isolation and career revitalization.

WHAT HAPPENS IF I DO SOMETHING WRONG?

The good news is that missteps along the way while using this model are usually not fatal. Learning a new model takes time and practice. As emerging solution-focused practitioners, we can trip up, get up, and start over; as long as we have a good relationship with students as a base, we can usually manage to carry on without having done any damage. Students let us know when we are off base as long as we have a strong radar for the clues. If we ask an exception question (described later in this chapter) before a student feels a connection with us, the question may be ignored or the students may scoff or rebuff us in some way. The typical student response to a misstep will be to reignite his or her problem-saturated story. Consider this a chance to regroup and start again more slowly by first working on the relationship and building on student strengths.

TECHNIQUES AND STRATEGIES OF SOLUTION-FOCUSED COUNSELING

In the following section, you will learn some of the techniques and strategies of a solution-focused approach. When implementing the following set of techniques with an individual or group, resist any tendency to cling to techniques instead of establishing meaningful relationships. Start with the relationship and build from there.

Pretreatment Change

As a practitioner new to this method, the process of starting the first discussion can seem daunting. Experienced practitioners may find that their typical openers (e.g., having students in a group on divorce discuss how they first learned their parents were getting divorced) are not consistent with a solution-focused approach. One way to start a solution-focused group discussion is by introducing the concept of pretreatment change.

In the late 1980s, solution-focused therapists who worked at the Milwaukee Brief Family Therapy Center noticed that clients often made changes in the desired direction between the time the appointment was scheduled and the first meeting. Michele Weiner-Davis (Weiner-Davis, deShazer, & Gingerich, 1987) and others began routinely asking clients the following question:

> Many times people notice in between the time they make the appointment for therapy and the first session that things already seem different. What have you noticed about your situation? (p. 306)

Results of their study indicated that 66 percent of their clients could note some positive changes. This was seen as getting a head start on the process of developing solutions.

Most students referred to a group will be aware of the focus of the meetings prior to the first encounter. Asking what each person has noticed that is different has potential to start a conversation about things that are a bit better or less problematic. When that happens (and it will not happen all the time), we are in the enviable position of starting with positive momentum and a certain hopefulness that problems can be solved.

If we ask a group what has changed and we get a flat *nothing* (and an implied *are you nuts?*), we can move on without skipping a beat. It will be like seeding a garden when we throw out questions; some will root and others will not. That should not be a surprise to us. Our job is to keep seeding—but to do so with intention, not randomly. Pretreatment change is not a critical conversation, but it is wonderful when it works out well.

When the pretreatment question does not work, it is worth paying attention to the circumstances. We may have an opportunity to learn something that could help us with future planning.

- Is there one influential person in the group who immediately negated the question and made it difficult for others to disagree? If so, we will need to think about power balance in the group. We will also probably need to work on ways for individuals to find a voice to disagree amicably.
- Did the leader ask the pretreatment question too soon? When students give us that deer-in-the-headlights look, we know our timing is off. It may be a group that is slow to warm or that lacks confidence. We may need to slow our pace and introduce the question later in the meeting once more security is established. In any case, the fact that the intervention did not work as intended can be important information about group dynamics if we are tuned in to them.

Setting Goals and Developing a Future Focus

Goals have an essential role when working from a solution-focused perspective. The goals are completely transparent. They are determined by the student—even if it takes some negotiating with the student to arrive at the goals. Students are far more likely to remain invested in goals they create. In more traditional models of psychotherapy, the client may have a goal in seeking therapy, but the clinician sometimes has another set of goals that become the *real* focus of treatment.

In this model, a goal is not about how to make the problem go away. When working with a group of high school students, a student may initially state that her goal is to be less depressed. From a solution-focused perspective, this is not a workable goal. We need to know what the student will *do* when she is less depressed. Goals can be quite simple. She can decide she will be less depressed when she joins her friends for lunch on Fridays. This is a practical goal that could lead to a useful conversation about what it would take to get to that Friday lunch. Once the desired behaviors are revealed, we are in a position to make goals she can work *toward* rather than ones she must work away from. Goals are about something that will be different in the future, what it will be like when the problem is solved.

Goals need to be concrete, measurable, and stated positively. Let's consider another example: In a group on social skills for third graders, Carlos says he wants his brother to be nicer to him. With this stated goal, we have two issues to address. First, a goal cannot be about what someone else needs to do to make his life work better; the goal must be about Carlos, the only person over whom he ever really has control. Second, to develop a sensible goal with Carlos, we must ask about the kind of relationship he *wants* to have with his brother. We know a little about what he does not want, but we will need to pinpoint what he is aiming for. We might ask about the times in the past when he has had the kind of relationship he desires. Our questions direct the conversation toward getting Carlos to envision what he wants and then strategizing about how to get there.

The Miracle Question

A very specific way to work on goal development with students is to ask the miracle question. Our guy Carlos is a good candidate for the miracle question because it may help him more clearly formulate the relationship he would like to have with his brother. The technique was developed by deShazer (1988) and has been adapted here.

So let me ask you this. . . .

   Suppose you went to bed tonight, and while you were sleeping a miracle happened and the problems that brought you here today disappeared. How would you know that the problems had disappeared? What would you notice that tells you a miracle happened?

Many students respond to this question by looking flummoxed. It is so out of their experience to think this way. They came to you with a problem and now you are asking about miracles! *What kind of nutty counselor are you, anyway?* The delivery on this question is important. If we sound too much like the tooth fairy and present the question in a perky, singsong fashion, students will wonder why we did not choose to teach preschool instead. If the presentation is conversational and demonstrates curiosity we have a better chance of engaging most students. Even then it takes work to get the conversation going. Students will not erupt with a ready-made vision. Michael Durrant (1995) suggested that it takes at least twenty minutes of conversation with a miracle question to really get somewhere; that may be a conservative estimate.

Some students will find it easy to work with you on developing a vision for the problem-free state. Others will reject the whole miracle idea as too much imaginary foo-foo. There are alternatives. It is possible to get to the same goal information by dropping the miracle idea and restating the question in more straightforward language.

So, once the problem is gone, what will your life be like and how will you know the problem is history?

It is always important for us to know our participants and make necessary adjustments. Some students will need a slightly more irreverent approach, and some will need a somewhat more playful approach. As counselors, we take on different personas based on the needs of the diverse students we serve and adjust our language accordingly.

In the case of Carlos, he was able to respond enthusiastically to the miracle question. His first big idea was about what his brother should do—again! With a little redirection, he was able to spell out the kind of brotherly relationship that he needs. He was clear about wanting to be his brother's friend, to have more fun and fight less, to spend less time being sent to their rooms . . . and then he proceeded to list *all* the things his brother could do to be a better friend. With a little redirection, again, Carlos was able to talk about the things he could do that would be friendly. He could share his electronic games, and he could stop tattling. He had some other ideas, but it was a slippery slope back to all the great things his brother should do. The leader needs to be patient and persistent. We are, after all, asking Carlos to make a big shift from blaming others to being more self-directed. This process takes time and repetition.

As the leader redirects Carlos a couple of times, others in the group have the benefit of a little training on goals; it gets easier for them to see that their goals need to be about themselves and not about other people. When some students have a grasp of the idea that goals need to be about what they can do (and not what others can do), we can use the group for support; if a student makes a goal statement about what someone else should do, the leader is now in a position to ask the whole group *Do you think that would work?* They can arrive at the conclusion that *they cannot control others* on their own.

In a 1996 study on a solution-focused group with middle schoolers, Rebecca LaFountain and others (LaFountain, Garner, & Eliason) used a traditional form of the miracle question during the second session of the series of group meetings. When a student's response described a miracle that could not become reality, the counselor worked with him or her and reformulated the question using the factors that were possible as the focus. Since the youngster in the dialogue, Casey, was not able to bring his

> **Follow-up to the Miracle Question**
>
> *What small part of the miracle you describe is already happening?*
>
> *What will be the first clue that this miracle has happened?*
>
> *What will you be doing that's different?*
>
> *Who will be the first to notice that this miracle happened?*
>
> *Who will be the most surprised?*

brother back to life, he created a helpful alternative. "I thought that since I'm in scouts, it might help me forget about it [brother shooting himself] and since I'm in here [the group] it might help me get it out of my mind. Not totally, but mostly out of my mind" (p. 4). Casey's goal can be inferred from the brief dialogue and was probably discussed more fully in the meeting. Casey wants to stop thinking about his brother so much. Now we have a goal. From a solution-focused perspective, the next step might be to discover what he is already doing during the times he is not thinking about his brother so much. Questions along this line are called *exception questions* and are discussed next.

Exceptions to the Problem

As we know from Assumption 3, problems do not happen all the time—even though it may seem that way to an embattled parent. The defiant teenager has moments of cooperation, maybe even cheerfulness. The shy first grader has times when he is able to respond to a peer, even if he is not yet initiating a conversation. There are times when a struggling student does get his homework done and turned in, even if it is rare or late. When problems are seen as omnipresent, we hear a lot of *always* and *never*. The problem becomes very large. It looms. It seems unmanageable, maybe unnerving, like a dark cloud over everything. By the time students, parents, and teachers seek out our consultation, they believe they have tried everything. They hope we have one more trick but clearly communicate that they are not counting on it.

What sounds like a very tall order turns out to be much smaller in reality. We engineer an about-face, reorienting the client to different aspects of his or her situation. As a solution-focused practitioner, our goal is to highlight the times the problem is *not* occurring because it is during these nonproblematic times that we will find the solution. We ask questions about exceptions to the problem . . . but slowly. People need to feel heard and understood before we begin our queries about exceptions. When we ask exception questions too soon, our clients usually just continue with the problem story. Sometimes, however, we can lose credibility by asking exception questions too early, so it is a good practice to carefully weigh our options and timing.

When clients come to the realization that the problem does not happen all the time, it usually comes as a relief. We create a space between the problem behavior and the nonproblem behavior when we ask about exceptions to the problem. The problem's stranglehold is loosened and there is more maneuverability in the system.

To examine this technique more closely, let's look at Raphael, a middle school student who struggles to complete his math homework. Instead of focusing on all the times Raphael failed to do his homework, we shift the focus to the times he actually got it done. By recognizing that Raphael turns in his work some of the time, we have something to build on. It is encouraging.

In addition to being encouraging for both students and parents, there is a very specific reason for this shift in focus. The times he failed to turn in his math homework do not give us any information about how to make the situation better; all we are left with is the default model. But the times he *did* turn in his math are ripe with information about how he can be successful. By carefully dissecting the circumstances, support, attitude, skill base, opportunity—anything related to how he got his math done— we have the blueprint for success in the future.

> **Exception Questions for Raphael**
>
> *How did you manage to get your homework turned in last week?*
>
> *What was different that made it easier to get it done?*
>
> *How did you resist the temptation to just ignore it?*

These exceptions to the dominant story about Raphael become the scaffolding for a new story. Whatever worked in the past needs to be repeated or refashioned in some way. If it worked doing homework with a friend, then maybe a buddy system or a homework club will help. If having access to his father netted more homework, then a regular check-in time with his dad may be the answer.

Exception questions can be used very effectively in groups. Once students are mildly acculturated to this way of thinking, they sometimes ask exception questions of each other. This becomes a peak moment for any counselor! I experienced this firsthand during the fourth session with a group of high school girls. Margaret, a sixteen-year-old, was rambling on about how much she hated her mother and how unfair she was when another student casually said, "So, is it always that bad? Sometimes I can't stand my mother, but sometimes she is OK." Margaret came to a screeching halt, looked a little dazed, and was temporarily speechless. I could almost see a text message running across her brain that said, "*I never thought of it like that.*" Margaret let go of her "evil mother" story and seemed to enjoy talking about times when she and her mother had fun.

The student intervention happened just moments ahead of when I would have asked a similar question, but it was so much more effective that the question came from the group. Once a group culture is established, this kind of student intervention is not as rare as one might think. When we work from a theoretical model, we provide a continuity of experience to students that they may absorb unconsciously. The net result can be students asking exception questions without being particularly aware of it. The power of the group cannot be overestimated.

We learn volumes about how to help students, parents, and teachers by asking well-timed exception questions. There is, however, one group for whom this technique has more limited use. This technique does not work as well with younger kids because the concept of exceptions seems difficult to grasp. Piaget would know why! It is likely a cognitive

> **Exception Questions for Margaret**
>
> *Even though you and your mom are on each other's nerves now, what was different about the times when you used to get along? What was that like? What did you do together that you enjoyed?*
>
> *Tell us about the last time you and your mother shared a good laugh together.*

and/or developmental issue. Younger children will fumble around trying to figure out what you want without grasping the notion. Rather than pursuing this kind of conversation with younger children, it is more effective to do more strength building, an issue we will discuss next.

Amplify and Build on Success

Most children are fortunate enough to have someone applauding and noting early successes such as learning names and then letters and numbers, tying those shoes, and riding a two wheeler. They learn to take more risks and have more successes, get more applause. Success breeds success. Unfortunately, the reverse is also true. As counselors, most of the kids we see have not enjoyed as much success.

John Gottman's (1995) extensive research on successful couples indicated that we need approximately five positive interactions with our partner to offset any one criticism. This ratio is the bare minimum for functioning successfully in a marriage. These positive interactions are like money in the bank and become a buffer against harsher conversations. We do not have the same carefully calculated information on children and teens, but it is a safe bet that students need to experience abundant success and develop their own buffer since they live in a world that will provide plenty of humbling experiences.

Wow, how did you do that? is a question that can be asked of a kid making pancakes, stacking blocks, reading a book, or learning to drive a car. Most of us have a strong need to be acknowledged and appreciated, and that's not a bad thing. We naturally want to do more of the things we think we do well. Conversely, we often eliminate the things we do not do well. When we take careful note of the things students do well, even if it is a fledgling effort, we are setting in motion a pattern likely to be repeated, a pattern likely to be improved by repetition. We can experience dry patches without shriveling up if we have enough of a success buffer.

Think of world-class athletes. Most have enjoyed success and applause along the way. Think of little class athletes! A coach addresses the stunned second graders following their first loss. In a pep talk, a good coach will focus on what a great team they are and how well they played. A brilliant coach will note specific things each child did well during the game to highlight success. Even in what looks like failure, it is important to look for strengths.

Walter and Peller (1992) told a great story about a pitcher for the Chicago Cubs who was in the middle of a slump and feeling demoralized. Determined to improve his performance, the pitcher went to the film room, pulled out footage of his most recent games, and carefully analyzed all the things he had done wrong. Late in the evening, the coach happened upon him and asked what he was doing. The pitcher explained that he was trying to figure out how to turn around his pitching and get back to where he had been previously. The coach quickly flipped off the projector and told him that this was a great idea, but that he was looking at the wrong films. The coach retrieved the films from times the pitcher had been a smashing success. These were the films to watch, to envision, mentally practice, and experience success—this was the way to turn his game around. Looking at the flawed performances was only helping him practice his mistakes. But success is another story. Success has an amazing way of duplicating itself.

> Sometimes we need to search high and low for strengths in our most challenging students. A colleague who is irrepressibly strength based in her work shared a moment when even she was stretched to the max. In a conversation with a student that did not go particularly well, she confessed that the only strength she could pin down for sure was "nice breathing." There are moments!

The importance of success takes on a kind of urgency when it comes to junior high students; they are in a class all their own. There are days when it is difficult to recognize them as human beings and days when they are downright adorable. But one thing is fairly constant: They are pretty hard on each other. The insecurity young people experience while emerging from childhood into full-blown adolescence takes its toll on the average student and can be an unmerciful experience for less confident kids. This is the period of development when it is crucial to have that buffer in the bank, that stockpile of past successes. It is also an important time to make generous deposits. Teachers and parents can make regular deposits, but the ones that double or triple in value are from peers. For this reason, group counseling is particularly well-suited for middle school students.

Questions That Build on Strengths

Lots of kids your age wouldn't have any idea how to do that. How did you figure it out?

If I understand what you are saying, each time you tried to do it, you got a little better. But it wasn't easy. You had to stick with it. How did you develop the courage to keep at it?

You have lots of temptations, things you would like to do, but somehow don't. How did you get to be the kind of person who can count on himself so often?

It sounds to me like you gave your friend some good advice. Who else besides you and me knows about this special talent you have?

What is it about you that makes kids want to be your friend and spend time with you?

In group counseling at any age level, amplifying success means we notice, appreciate, and validate things students are already doing that make their lives work. We might design a group meeting around things they are good at, special interests, heroes, or hobbies. When the conversation reverts to the problems and deficits (as it inevitably will), we might ask, *How have you managed to keep things from getting worse?* or *What's kept you from giving up?* Questions such as these put students in the position of describing strengths, exactly where you want them to be. In a group, everyone benefits when one student talks about an ability to bounce back from adversity. They model for each other a capacity for resourcefulness. They have an opportunity to piggyback on each others' strengths. They share road maps, all pioneers in their own ways.

Reframing

Reframing is an art form. It is the ability to transform something a student tells us so that new meaning is attached. It is the ability to take something that has a negative valence and make it appear to have a positive or neutral valence. The goal is to help students see something differently, to free them from being encumbered by the negativity of their interpretation. Reframing a situation or relationship does not help a student know what to do, but it does free the student to think more creatively about possibilities. When done by the masters of therapy, it has a magical quality and leaves those of us newer to the field wondering, *How did they do that?*

Milton Erickson was an extraordinary therapist and the ultimate genius at reframing. He is also the "father" of family therapy and was an early influence in the development of what would become solution-focused counseling. Stories about his work are legendary. He shared a story about one of his clients that is a perfect demonstration of reframing and the inherent power of this technique. The following is an adaptation of that story, as discussed in Haley (1973).

A young woman sought an appointment with Erickson following the death of both her parents. As an only child, she was alone in the world and feeling depressed. She had a steady job, but did not experience much satisfaction in her work. She had few friends and no love interest. She believed she would never marry as she looked so homely. She drew this conclusion based largely on the gap she had between her two front teeth.

As Erickson and this young woman got to know each other, she revealed that she had considering killing herself. Erickson, no doubt, assessed for safety and must have concluded that she was not a danger to herself. He did not argue with her thought that perhaps it would be better to be dead than alive. He took a completely different tact and requested that she complete certain tasks. He persuaded her to take some money from her bank account and have one last fling; she was directed to go on a shopping spree. She protested, but eventually agreed. She returned the next week having made several purchases and looking mildly pleased.

As their conversations continued, the woman talked a bit more about her work and began to mention a man she had seen at the water cooler. They had never spoken, but Erickson surmised that she was interested in him. Erickson devised a remarkable task. He instructed her to go home and learn to shoot water out between the gap in her two front teeth a distance of six feet, and not to return until she could do it successfully for him in the office. She protested, but eventually agreed. When she returned, she took a gulp of water and demonstrated her newfound skill for Erickson who must have delighted in her accomplishment. During the conversation, he learned that the man at the water cooler was appearing there regularly and she was beginning to coordinate her breaks with his appearances.

The next task was even more challenging. This time she was directed to go to the water cooler; when the man appeared, she was to take a gulp of water, take a step back, and spray him with water. This time she protested vigorously, but somehow Erickson got her to agree. During the meeting that followed, she recounted with pleasure how she had sprayed him with water and run back to her desk. The next day when they both arrived at the water cooler, he was armed with a water pistol, and a romance ensued!

This quintessential Erickson story captures many of the elements of a solution-focused approach. Erickson did not argue with her idea that life might not be worth living; she was, after all, the expert on her problem. Instead, he directed her down another path; if what you are doing is not working, *do something different.* Without many exceptions to the problem of feeling depressed to build on, he helped her create some. She enjoyed having some new clothes and took the task of shooting water from between her front teeth seriously. It simply is not as easy to feel totally depressed while you are learning to shoot water from between your front teeth. He built on her success with earlier tasks until he was able to spring the last really hard one on her. But it is his reframing of the gap that is his real genius. He took the source of her most significant complaint, this seemingly ugly gap, and turned it into a weapon to fight off depression and a way to win at love. The gap became her friend. The gap was completely reframed.

Erickson could never explain how he did what he did. He argued that all his interventions were individual because he had never run into a general client. Indeed. But we can take a little therapeutic inspiration from his work. We can take the things students, teachers, or parents say to us and help create a new perspective. To illustrate how this might look at the school level, here is an adaptation of a story shared by a former graduate student (adapted from D. Queen, personal communication, 1999).

Scott, age eight, was mightily distressed, as his younger brother repeatedly got into his room and made a mess of his things. The counselor commented about how curious the little boy must be about his older brother, and simply wondered aloud if the younger brother looked up to him. After listening for some time and empathizing with how upsetting this situation must be, she said to him, "*It must be hard to be his hero.*" As she recounts the story, the boy stared at her briefly and simply agreed. Suddenly, it was as though the previous conversation had never occurred and he began to strategize about how to work things out with his sibling. He decided on a sign and picture, which he promptly made for his door. When the picture was on the door, it meant "do not disturb." But he also cooked up a plan to invite his brother into his room to play. He volunteered that he would do this regularly since younger brothers have to learn *stuff* from their older brothers!

The counselor was able to take the younger brother's behavior and transform it into hero worship. Instead of being a victim of his younger brother, Scott was freed to step into the mentor role. He was also relieved of the angst attached to the situation.

We are also reframing when we take the descriptions of students that teachers and parents give us and soften them a little. When the teacher talks about the student as annoyingly hyperactive, we might refer to the same student as *overly enthusiastic*. When a parent refers to her daughter as completely stubborn, we can reflect that back as *having a mind of her own*. When a student says the teacher is out to get him, we could comment that the teacher sounds *invested in your success*. In each case, we have lightened the load of the more negative description. We have created a little space for possibilities to emerge.

Scaling Questions

Scaling questions are a form of progress monitoring; they allow the student and counselor to reflect on the status of the counseling situation at the moment and on any changes over time. This simple strategy is quite useful, and the straightforwardness is refreshing to students. They can communicate a good bit of information without having to say a lot. The wording can be modified for the situation and for the age level of the student. In basic form, the scaling question is as follows:

On a scale from 0 to 10, with 10 being the best it could be and 0 being the worst it could be, how would you rate your situation now?

If a student looks puzzled, it is good to add that 5 would be about average. Sometimes this added information provides clarity. Students seem to enjoy the process and usually find some satisfaction in communicating the information. It is possible to add that there are no wrong or right answers, but that is seldom needed.

You sound very clear about your rating. What has happened that led you to pick that number?

What's the highest you have ever been? The lowest?

When you were at your lowest point, how did you get it moving back up again?

What would you say is your best technique for moving up on the scale?

Are there things you can do that have a pretty good chance of taking you lower on the scale?

What kind of things help keep you at your ideal rating?

Like the miracle question, responses to scaling questions need follow-up. Sometimes we need to add a little *spin*. To a response of "5," we might say, *Oh, you are halfway there.* To a response of "6," we could comment that it is above average. Other questions are designed to elaborate on the information. To a response of "2," it may be appropriate to comment that the situation sounds like a big challenge right now; a follow-up question might be to ask what it would take to increase the rating by just one number. Another possible line of questions involves self-assessment, such as the following: *What makes your situation a 4 right now?* Additional discussion can involve developing an "audience" for the situation; we can inquire about people in their lives who might notice or be supportive of changes, or even people who might be surprised by changes.

Scaling questions become a record of progress over time. When asked to rate their present circumstances, it can be useful to remind students of a previous rating (e.g., *Last time we talked, you were at a 4. Where are you now?*). Students like it when we remember what they say, and the process of rating helps them appreciate that their situation is not stagnant—it can and does change.

Children under seven years of age may need some adaptations with scaling questions. Their capacity for making relative judgments and working with numbers in this way is not fully developed. A concrete aid that is a series of five faces with expressions ranging from *extremely happy* to *extremely sad* can be substituted for numbers. The directions are altered to reflect this change. Children can simply circle the face that describes their experience at the moment. This concrete aid can also be used with the follow-up questions and saved for later comparisons.

There is one potential liability with this technique. In our enthu-siasm to be helpful, we are vulnerable to asking leading questions that prompt for specific ratings. This is what we want to avoid:

Last time we talked you were at a 4. How much have you come up from that? How much would you say the situation has improved?

Are you feeling better?

This kind of forced improvement can easily backfire with students getting overly attached to the lack of progress, more attached than they may really feel. Since we apparently did not hear what they were saying, they now hold more tightly to their position to make the point. For these reasons, it is important to maintain a neutral stance when asking scaling questions; that way, both students and counselor will get more accurate data and avoid any unnecessary power strug-gles about the information.

When we take a neutral position about ratings on scaling ques-tions, we demonstrate that we are open to the possibility that ratings may go down . . . things may get worse. Students appreciate seeing that we will not collapse or give up on them when they deliver bad news. At times like this, it is important not to try and talk them out of it. We accept what they say; they are the experts. Our ability to accept a drop in a rating may be quite validating. Sometimes the sit-uation has not really gotten worse, but the student has just worked up more nerve to tell you how bad it really is. Either way, we want to reinforce the students' ability to be forthcoming with their assess-ment and start the conversation wherever they are.

Scaling questions are used in a variety of ways in group counsel-ing. Starting a group meeting with a general scaling question can be a good way to check in with each member and for members to become aware of each other quickly and easily. We might ask, *On a scale of 0 to 10, what kind of rating would you give your life today?* Students may wish to add a little about how they arrived at their rat-ing; this can be helpful information for both the leader and the members. However, it is important not to overfocus on students with low ratings. If every time a student gives a rating of 2 the leader and others express sympathy and take deliberate actions to prop the person up, we are likely to get more ratings of 2 over time. It is good to offer acknowledgment without embellishment. If resilience is what we are cultivating, then students who give high ratings need air time to explain how life can be so good. In the choices we make and the interactions in the group, our purpose is to amplify success. What we chose to emphasize, and what we do not, becomes influential.

There are times, however, when it would be sensible to attend to several low ratings at the start of a group. *I can see that many of you are not feeling so great today. I wonder if it would be helpful to have a conversation about the issues or would it be more helpful to put it aside?* This gives students a choice that is usually seen as respectful. This should be used judiciously. It is best to avoid promoting a culture based on drama; it can be a bottomless pit. However, it may be necessary to spend time discussing the issues if there has been a crisis or bad news that affects most of the group. When you are running a group after lunch and there has been a fight, there is no point in trying to move on with your agenda until this has been dealt with in some way. Trying to change the subject when everyone is fired up just does not work!

Scaling questions can also be used on an individual basis to assess progress on goals. During a group meeting, students might rate where they are in dealing with their parents' divorce. Each student does an individual rating. The conversation that follows is about how they arrived at that rating today and what they plan to do in the future to shift the rating. Students can offer each other suggestions based on their experience. Starting the conversation with a rating scale gives the discussion substance, something to hold on to, and a way to make sense of the tangled web of thoughts and feelings.

SUMMARY

The techniques and strategies associated with solution-focused brief counseling are like jumper cables for the brain. They have an electrifying quality and an easy appeal to many practitioners. In this chapter, we examined several techniques that can be used successfully in groups: pretreatment change, goal setting, the miracle question, exception questions, building on success, reframing, and scaling questions. With practice, this way of working becomes invigorating and rewarding as it produces change in a positive environment.

Using any of these techniques effectively is based on first developing a solid relationship with students. Without a solid relationship, techniques can become gimmicks. With a solid relationship as a foundation, techniques and strategies used effectively can help transform the lives of our students.

CHAPTER FOUR

Adapting Group Curriculum Material

General Principles

In this chapter and the chapter that follows, you will learn how to use the assumptions and techniques of solution-focused brief counseling (SFBC) to adapt group curriculum material and create the kind of blockbuster activities that make you glad you decided to lead more groups! As discussed in previous chapters, the assumptions are the foundation for this approach and they guide our decisions; therefore, much of what is discussed in these chapters is not necessarily *what* activities you will lead but rather *how* you will lead them.

There are several features that make an activity consistent with a solution-focused approach, and these features will be consistent regardless of the activity you are leading. Some activities are so inconsistent with a solution-focused approach that the activity does not merit the effort to adapt it. However, many activities need only minor modification. This chapter will explore how to choose an activity, how to make it your own, and how to make the environment safe enough for the activity to be a vehicle for change.

CHOOSING AN ACTIVITY

As practitioners leading groups in schools, there is no shortage of material to choose from when we plan a group. The downside, however, is that most activities are not designed with a theoretical orientation in mind. For those interested in leading groups from a solution-focused perspective, that means it will be necessary to convert an existing activity into something more closely consistent with solution-focused thinking. This is actually not difficult; it just means we need to set aside the time to carefully review activities and make modifications. We will not be able to do the "10-minute dash"—zoom down the hall, grab our group curriculum book, collect the students, take a deep breath, and begin the group by turning to page 58—and still expect things to go swimmingly. Preparation is always in order, and converting activities into something more solution focused requires forethought. The following is a summary of the general principles for choosing material that will be appropriate for a solution-focused group.

Do This	Avoid This
Provide opportunities to highlight student strengths	Promoting conversations about how things got to be so bad
Orient the discussion toward the present and desired future	Focusing on the history of the problem
Get mightily curious about the solution	Getting overly interested in the problem

Provide Opportunities to Highlight Student Strengths

Solution-focused practitioners look for activities that give students a chance to shine, to show what they know and impress the group, themselves, and us. This means we seize any opportunity to notice resources and support positive momentum. Most often, the things we notice and comment on are small. Students do not need to triumph over adversity in order to get our attention. Our acknowledgment can be simple, such as the following comment made to a second grader: *I appreciate that you remembered whose turn it is . . . it shows that you are really paying attention.*

In a social skills group, we notice behaviors that support friendship skills and likeability. It might sound like this: *How did you learn to be such a careful listener?* or *You seem to have an excellent ability to remember what others say. How do you do that?* This is fairly straightforward. In a group on grief, the orientation continues to be strength based; the focus is on ways to cope effectively with whatever thoughts and feelings the participants are experiencing. When students talk about how they did *not* cope well (and they will), the leader will be empathetic with their challenges *and* carefully attuned to any strengths—times when they managed with a bit more ease, let someone be soothing, or perhaps when they slept just a little better. We might ask, *How did you know it was a good time to let your dad comfort you?* or *What did you do to keep the thoughts you didn't want in your head away as you tried to fall asleep?*

When Strengths Are Hard to Find

This concept may be easier to imagine in some kinds of groups than in others, but as solution-focused practitioners we are relentless in our pursuit of strengths—even when those strengths may be somewhat unconventional. For example, students who meet to talk about anger management may arrive at the observation that it is fun to get angry, to really blow their top. Keen observers can see how much control they have over others when they are really angry. So how do you look for strengths in the midst of this conversation?

This is a conversation that may make us uneasy because it runs counter to conversations we generally see as acceptable with students. Will students mistake our curiosity about the effects of anger as supporting their right to get angry in an uncontrolled way? It depends on our response. The key seems to be that we accept their observations without condoning their behavior. When students talk about how fun it is to get angry, a potential strength is their ability to be aware of other people even as they appear out of control. We can use this power of observation and tilt it toward more acceptable ways of interacting: *I see you notice how your anger makes people react to you. How do you express being unhappy about something and not make someone mad at you?*

Liabilities

When we are building on strengths, the danger is that we can sound too Pollyannaish, too *super-duper*—delivery is everything.

With younger children, we can be enthusiastic and effervescent, but older students require a slightly more offhand approach, more distant and less enveloping. When we get too enthusiastic with older students, they are quick to disown the resource we are appreciating, as though we have just given them a suffocating case of claustrophobia! This kind of exchange may end up inadvertently negating the very strength we are highlighting.

Orient the Discussion Toward the Present and Desired Future

Most of us have some childhood memory of sniveling and whining to a parent or teacher who dutifully responded with a sympathetic *"Tell me what happened."* As we get older, we become increasingly better as historians of random injustices suffered at the hands of a sibling, a classmate, or a grouchy grandparent. We have a story to tell, and since we do our own editing, it usually makes us look good! This exchange, modified as appropriate, is a regular occurrence in most of our lives. We tell our story and receive comfort, reassurance, maybe some advice. As a typical way of expressing ourselves and relating to other important people in our lives, it works well; our needs are met, and we move on.

However, some students do not move on. They get ensnared and repeat the same problematic behavior without knowing how to do something different. These are the students who get referred to counselors. When they repeatedly tell us what happened, they become entrenched and have fewer prospects for creating lasting change. These are the students who need our help getting out of the past (where the options have not proved favorable) and into the future, where there are possibilities for doing something different.

In our group meetings, we fold a future orientation into most activities by having follow-up questions that ask deliberately about the desired future and the present choices that are consistent with that future. Looking through a strength-based lens with a future orientation, we can quickly reject activities that prompt students to talk about how things got to be so awful, as this typically results in a conversation in which the students discuss being victimized. Students will naturally talk about their bad experiences, but from an SFBC orientation, we do not structure the activity to pull out that material.

In addition, specific activities orient the conversation toward the future, such as asking students what they see themselves doing five, ten, and fifteen years from now. We follow up by asking, *What will it take to make that desired outcome happen?* When one teenager says that he sees himself in jail or dead (and this will happen), notice how quickly we formulate a mental response with something that negates this gruesome possibility. It is troubling to hear students talk this way; it is almost instinctual to say something reassuring and validating and try to get the student to take a different position. This is a mistake. When we take this protective approach, we are picking up a rope and starting a tug of war with them. What if we stay curious and ask, instead, *What makes you think you will be in jail?* We may hear some bluster, but we will likely have an opportunity to say something like, *Well, suppose you decided you did not want to go to jail, what would you be doing now that would help you stay out of jail in the future?* Students will give us all the history on why jail seems likely, but this history does not help them figure out what to do differently. It is not until we are talking about the future that there is a chance to carve out a different life story.

Get Mightily Curious About the Solution

Sometimes students in a group make an offhand comment about something they did that they see as unimportant, even though the behavior they mention actually was a bull's eye on the solution trajectory. It is as though the desired outcome was so uncommon that it was easy to disregard. It was a fluke. For example, a student might note that when he or she arrived home from school yesterday, the typical fight over when to do homework did not occur. Students may make this kind of comment in passing and move on to something else. But if the issue on the table is how to get your parents to back off, this student has just had the kind of interaction that is definitely worth repeating.

As group leaders, our job at that moment is to quickly redirect the conversation back to the homecoming interaction. We might say, *Really? You got home, greeted your mother, and it was pleasant? You two didn't tangle? Really? What did you do differently? What did you talk about instead of homework?* When we get really curious, students often look at us like we have had a brain freeze and are making much ado about nothing. This is where working from a theoretical orientation really pays off. We are purposeful and directed in our line of questions. Even if the student can answer few of them, we are making our point. They have more control than they may be assuming, and all the students in the group are getting that signal loud and clear. *What were you like when you walked in the door? What kind of mood were you in? Who said hello first? What difference did it make? What small step can you take to repeat that?* When we are more interested in the solution than the problem, we are leading the parade toward the desired future and helping to create the blueprint for a happier life.

MAKE IT YOUR OWN

Counseling is a creative process with a vitality born of the many interactions we have with students. We put our personality stamp on the approach we use and it slowly morphs into something that runs in our blood stream. As we make it our own, we no longer have to think about everything we do in counseling—it becomes second nature. This takes time and practice.

Do This	Avoid This
Examine your own strengths	Leading activities that make you uncomfortable

As educators, we want students to know, appreciate, and use their strengths, but we can get squeamish when asked to discuss our own strengths. Why is that? The teasing or criticism doled out for bragging at an early age may be to blame, but if we are to get students to connect with their strengths, it seems prudent for us to do the same.

Make a list of your strengths, talk about it with a friend, and discuss how you think you use your strengths in your work and daily life. Consider what strengths you would like to develop in the future and what you will do to develop in that way. For ideas, visit the University of Pennsylvania's Questionnaires Center Web site (www.authentichappiness.sas.upenn.edu/questionnaires.aspx) and take the VIA Signature Strengths Questionnaire. There are several questionnaires available at this site and all are free. In addition to a score, you will have the opportunity to take the survey at later times and make comparisons. This is also a good activity to do with high school students, and there is a VIA Strengths Survey for Children.

Consider your strengths in relationship to leading group-counseling meetings. Some activities may not be a good fit for you. Be sure you are comfortable with what you are doing and the material you are using. When you force yourself to lead activities that are way outside your comfort zone, the results may not be what you hoped.

A couple of personal examples are in order here. I enjoy working with puppets and find them very effective with young children. This is not, however, true for everyone. Forcing yourself into an approach that does not match your style or your training will come across as stilted. Additionally, it is likely to make you nervous. This will not go unnoticed by students. When we look to students like we do not know what we are doing, it can heighten their insecurities and can lead to acting-out behavior.

Here is an example of something I avoid. I never do relaxation activities with students. There is plenty of research to support their effectiveness; I am just not the right person to lead this kind of activity. Perhaps if I had more training and experience, I would get there. But what that means for now is that I do not lead relaxation activities. So when you self-assess, if you find yourself squirming at the thought of leading a specific activity, consider modifying it or doing something else. There are many ways to accomplish your goal. Creativity counts!

> What kinds of activities are a natural fit for you? What kinds of activities make you uncomfortable? What alternatives can you come up with to accomplish the same thing?

CREATING A SAFE ENVIRONMENT

How safe did you feel at your first school dance? Many of us experienced an odd combination of excited and scared; others were terrified or mortified. Some of us never went! But for those who were able to show up, recall what made you feel comfortable. Someone you knew might have greeted you or you may have gone with a group. You might have known the music, maybe even the words. You could have been relieved to find that students danced in a group. Now, superimpose that same angst-relief scenario on group counseling. Our goal is to take the sting out of showing up and make it worth the participant's while to stay for the whole meeting, maybe even talk. Create a welcoming environment and students will show up for the next meeting too.

Do This	Avoid This
Evaluate the developmental level of the material in relation to the group	Assuming that the grade-level description matches your group
Make early activities neutral	Using activities that may require too much emotional risk in the early stage of the group
Check in with yourself	Having preconceived notions
Use humor	Using sarcasm

Developmental Level of the Group

Students feel comfortable when what you are talking about is seen as appropriate for their age. The fact that a book says "Grades 7 to 9" on the cover is not, however, a guarantee that it will match your middle school group. Picking activities that are developmentally appropriate usually requires modifying materials. If you are new to a district, or new to a school, observe in multiple classrooms to learn the culture of the school and the overall maturity and sophistication of the students. Knowing something about the assessment program in the state and the specific results in your school is also helpful.

If the majority of students are functioning a year or more below grade level academically, then you may need to adjust your material accordingly. Certainly, this is not always the case. There is not a direct correlation between maturity and academic performance. Similarly, you may have students who are psychologically minded or mature, and this group will require activities that are more sophisticated. When we ask a question that bombs, there is a window of opportunity for forgiveness—but not if we make the same mistake repeatedly. This issue merits consideration in our planning.

Make the Early Activities Neutral

Make the early activities nonthreatening and neutral so that the emotional atmosphere in the room is comfortable. The self-talk we want to generate in the minds of students as we ask them to do things in the early meetings is, *"Oh, I can do that; that's easy."* In the beginning, it is risky enough for some of them to show up, so our goal at this point is to make it fun. We want them to leave thinking, *"That wasn't so bad . . ."* or maybe even, *"I liked that."* This will increase the possibility that students are willing to show up next time!

The following scenario represents an increased challenge for the leader based on the subject matter, and this will really highlight the importance of starting a group in neutral territory. Imagine that you are leading a group at the secondary level on developing racial tolerance following some ethnically charged school events. The faculty has set a school goal of working toward appreciation of differences. One of the initial steps was to ask you to do a series of meetings with the students who are seen as leaders of the various groups who are at odds with one another. The outcome of your group discussions will become advisory to the administration and teachers. This issue calls for extremely careful planning as the topic can be quite volatile.

As you consider the first meeting agenda, you decide on a "name" activity as an opener but struggle picking a second activity. What would be neutral? Since music is often seen as a unifying force in teens, you decide on an activity that invites members to share their preferences for music groups. Red alert. You may have walked into a musical land mine! The differences between members of the group may be reflected in their choice of music; in this case, they also may feel competitive about which group has better music. This activity, which sounded so neutral and potentially unifying, could end up accentuating the very differences we were hoping to minimize. Back to the drawing board.

> What approach might you have taken to check out whether the music activity would work? What are your resources here?
>
> If you read the example about having groups on racial tolerance and found yourself feeling unequal to the task, what would you want to do in order to feel better prepared? What are your resources? What would be your first step?

Check In With Yourself

Sometimes our biases are so connected to our values and beliefs that we are blind to the power and influence they have over us. The trouble with blind spots is they are hard to see! For this reason, it is good practice to intentionally self-evaluate and consult with others. When we maintain an open and nondefensive posture in our collegial consultation, we have a chance to keep issues from ambushing us. We will review this issue in the case example below.

Case Example: Sixth Graders and Cliques

Let's look at solution-focused facilitation in action. Imagine leading a group of sixth-grade girls who are referred to you because the cliques that have developed in the class have led to outright bullying and ostracizing of some students. The teacher has tried class meetings with limited success. The principal hopes you can turn this dynamic around by meeting with a group of the worst offenders. Since you are new to the field, and in an effort to be helpful, the principal hands you a book on group activities to prevent bullying. You meet with the girls individually prior to any group meeting and it is easy to see they have little interest in any counseling and a flagrantly negative attitude about girls outside their group. This may be your worst nightmare! Just how is this group going to be strength based?

Check in with yourself. Before we tread any further, the most important first step may be an attitude adjustment for ourselves. We may need to reframe our position in relation to the girls. The principal's nudge, with book in hand, propels us right into "should" territory. It sounds like this: *Girls should be nice to each other. Girls shouldn't marginalize others. Girls should see the error of their ways.* All this mind chatter, even if unconscious, will set us up to approach the girls in lecture mode, which is not what we want from a solution-focused perspective. When we are in lecture-mode, it is hard to see strengths and it is not likely that we will see the girls as experts. Of course, the "shoulds" listed above make perfect sense; they just do not help us if what we are after is *change.* It all gets back to what we think about change. How can we create situations and conversations that promote change rather than cement the girls to their "better than thou" position?

The attitude we adopt in relation to these girls is pivotal, and luckily, we get to pick our attitude. The attitude we adopt will influence every move we make in the group and will be transparent to the girls. If we like them, they will know it; if we think they are mean and petty, they will know that too. We can like the student without condoning the behavior. But what is the configuration of an attitude that helps us get there? There are numerous possibilities, but the general goal is to soften any judgments we hold.

One possibility is to imagine the girls at a younger age. As kindergartners, it seems unlikely that these girls set out to marginalize others. Something got in the way as they got older. Perhaps they were left out of small things and learned to protect themselves by having a guaranteed group, a clique. Maybe some of them feel frightened that others will not like them unless they are part of an accepted in-group. Perhaps some of them go with the flow more out of habit than choice. Others may feel a need to be seen as special and this is the only way they are validated. This list of possibilities could be extended, but we arrive at the same point. We do not have to be right about how this problem developed; we just need to relinquish judgment so that we can be more effective with the girls. As solution-focused leaders, we adopt the attitude that puts us in the best possible position to promote change; in this case, it starts with seeing these girls as needing something that life has not yet provided—a safe enough place where they can be themselves without having to put others down to get there. This is something we can offer in a solution-focused counseling group.

Inventory student strengths. Now think about possible strengths for these students. It may come more easily now. Take a moment and generate a list of possible strengths for the girls. They will teach us what we need to know about them, but envisioning what we may find can help us prepare. With a more open attitude toward the girls, we are in a much better position to plan a group that will bring out the best in each of them and the best in the group as a whole.

> Possible strengths of sixth-grade girls: They really care about their friends and stick up for them. They are loyal. They help each other out. They know how to have fun together. They share their music. They treat each other with respect, including how they handle Facebook.

Use Humor

Humor can be a positive force in gentle doses. We all like to laugh. Humor that is playful and not edgy can bring a group together. However, even a hint of sarcasm, especially at the secondary level, will devastate a group. Sarcasm is risky under any circumstance; the tendency is to enjoy a laugh at someone else's expense. From an SFBC perspective, we undercut the expertise of another with this kind of humor. Secondary students will use sarcasm with each other; sometimes it is mostly stylistic, but it can be a destructive force. Students are more accustomed to hearing it from each other than from an adult, so it behooves us not to join sarcastic banter. In the early stages of a group, it may be best to just change the subject. In later sessions, when more trust is established, it may be possible to discuss the effects of sarcasm directly as long as the conversation is blameless and neutral.

SUMMARY

Activities from existing group plans can often be adapted to fit into an SFBC approach. In this chapter, the focus is on choosing an activity, making it your own, and creating a safe environment.

In choosing an activity, pick ones that allow students to see their own competence. The goal is to be generous with our acknowledgments and low-key in our delivery with secondary students. To lead an effective solution-focused group, we will want to amplify student competence rather than examine flaws, maintain a certain vigilance in our search for strengths, and notice these strengths out loud. This usually calls for a fair amount of redirection of the group because students are inclined to focus on the problem, the complaints, the woes, and the failed attempts. The payoff for leader persistence is conversations that build on strengths and students who begin to see themselves differently.

As we practice with a new model, we gradually make it our own. One day it suddenly happens—you realize you did not have to think about what to say next; it just happened and it was consistent with the chosen model. Our ability to be effective takes a giant leap forward on that day. There will, however, be activities or certain strategies that make us uncomfortable. When this happens, it is usually better to think of an alternate route to the same destination.

Last, if students do not feel safe in the group, we will not have the benefit of knowing what they really think. Efforts to be welcoming, friendly, and acknowledging pay off when the students return the next week. We do this by making the material age appropriate and beginning with neutral activities. Humor can be more divisive than uniting, especially in the early stages, so caution is advised. Preconceived notions can be shelved in favor of a mighty curiosity.

CHAPTER FIVE

Adapting Group Curriculum Material

Specific Strategies

W e know a spectacular group-counseling activity when we see one. It makes us wonder, causes us to reconsider, stretches our ideas and feelings, and is often just downright fun. The inclination is to repeat this great activity, modified as needed—to show others, to delight them. It is, after all, a great pleasure to lead an activity that participants find intriguing, mesmerizing, and expansive. Oh, would that all our group activities were so!

In addition to the general principles discussed in the last chapter, there are some specific adaptations for creating this type of blockbuster solution-focused activity. This chapter will examine three distinct aspects of solution-focused group material: group discussion, goal setting, and the role of questions. These are concrete methods for transforming activities into engaging experiences.

Group discussion refers to the subject matter of the meeting—the topic; it is *what* we plan to talk about along with the activities students will engage in to promote discussion. The second concept, *goal setting*, is central to solution-focused brief counseling (SFBC). The goals are created by the students and evaluated frequently. Last, *questions* function like a compass on the solution-focused map. Questions help us steer the course, jostle the homeostasis, and set in motion possibilities for change.

GROUP DISCUSSION

The topic of the meeting is based on the reason for referral. While there are some common themes (e.g., recovering from divorce, learning effective anger management, developing friendship skills), the possibilities for topics and activities are endless and vary according to the needs of students. No matter what the topic, the strategies below apply.

Do This	Avoid This
Review activities thoroughly	Being overly persuaded by the book title
Explore both sides of an issue	Asking leading questions
Attend to what may sound like unrelated ideas	Changing the subject

Review Activities Thoroughly

Do not be fooled by the book title. If bullying is the issue you want to solve, then a book that says bullying on the cover may provide relief—but it could be short lived. It may look like a gift from the gods, but it may turn out to be the activity book from hell! Review material carefully.

Let's use the example of the sixth-grade girls and cliques from the previous chapter to review the appropriateness of an activity. We have oriented ourselves to the group and we see its strengths. But what do we actually do with them? Could the book the principal loaned us on bullying be helpful? There may be activities that we can tweak and follow-up questions that can be carefully adapted to be solution focused. There are, however, some activities common to books on bullying that we **clearly want to avoid**:

1. Asking the girls how they would like it if others ostracized them. The misguided goal in this common approach may be an attempt to develop empathy, but it will only result in eye rolling, either directly to your face or behind your back.

2. Asking girls why they pick on others. As soon as *why* comes out of your mouth, you know you are in lecture mode.

3. Asking girls to plan an imaginary class party and develop games that would include everyone. This is a bit forced unless you have complete student buy-in.

4. Having the girls separate into pairs and make a list of all the disadvantages of having cliques. Discuss this as a whole group. The problem with this idea will be discussed in the next session; the short version is that this kind of discussion lacks balance.

5. Initiating a discussion on how to break up cliques at their school. This activity does rely on student expertise (their knowledge about cliques). What does this idea need to be solution focused and to have a better chance of working with this group? This idea only works if the girls are motivated to break up cliques.

> Which ideas from SFBC does each of these ill-fated conversations violate? (1) This is a shaming approach and not strength based. (2) Asking *why* questions is a setup for a lecture. (3) If you had buy-in and this was a terminating activity after several group meetings, it might work—especially if the group could actually have the party they plan for everyone. What is it about having the party that makes this idea work? (4) This idea lacks balance, so it may feel like another lecture (see the next section). (5) This idea needs at least some student buy-in. If the activity reflects the leader's goal and not the students', it may just provide students with a way to miss class time without changing anything.

Can you see elements of the default model running through these examples?

These kinds of suggested activities on bullying have clear limitations from a solution-focused perspective. It is easy to locate other activity guides that are thematically appropriate for your planned group and packed with activities. We may heave a sigh of relief at the prospect of solving the *What am I going to DO with this group?* issue, but our joy will be short-lived if we have neglected to carefully adapt the material. Buyers beware!

Imagine that the book on bullying from the principal gets rejected and so does every other activity we locate. The likely problem is the negativity of the presentation. Much of the time when we talk about bullying, it is with a clear eye toward wanting to prevent it and stop students in their tracks. The hope is that if students saw the disadvantages of their misguided behavior, they would make more enlightened choices. Basically, this approach is about *insight*—which is more psychodynamic than solution focused.

From an SFBC perspective, we want to work toward something rather than putting our energy into eradicating something undesirable. In this case, developing friendship skills is the antithesis of bullying and it may be a better starting point. The importance of working toward something is the reason that Examples 3 and 5 are a better bet than the others. When the referral issue is bullying, beginning a group by asking what they value in a friend is less likely to make students defensive. This conversation merits a long discussion and could include issues such as the following:

How do you know someone is your friend?

Have you ever lost a friend?

What's something you would never do to a friend?

What quality do you value most in your friends?

Is that different from when you were younger?

Have you ever had to break off a friendship?

Did you handle it as well as you would have liked?

What quality about you do you think others value in a friendship?

Following this more general conversation, the leader might use later meetings to shift the conversation slightly:

Do you have many friends or a few?

Has it always been that way?

What do you value in the group you are most connected to now?

How did you get connected to the group?

What are you able to do as a result of being in the group?

What effect do you think groups have on students in general?

What about your class?

Are there ever times when what the group wants is more important than what you want?

How do you handle that?

The intent is to examine the issue, rely on student expertise, avoid pressing a position, and listen. If you are meeting with a group of dedicated seventeen-year-old gang members, these kinds of questions might not provoke reconsideration, but with sixth-grade girls who are sorting out how to relate in their new social world, these kinds of questions can be quite provocative.

Explore Both Sides of an Issue

In a solution-focused counseling group, students can air their perspective even if that perspective is unpopular with most educators. This means that while our goal is to be strength based, it does not mean that all conversations need to be positive and all about the rosy side of life. In fact, it is important to give equal time to both sides of the issue. We do that when we ask, *How does that decision work* against *you?* followed by, *How does it work* for *you?* And because the student is the expert, follow up with, W*hat do you think is in your best interest?* This example works well at the secondary level.

At the elementary level, we might simplify by asking something roughly equivalent: *Tell us what you like about X,* followed by, *What don't you like about X?* So far this may sound all right; we are attending to both sides of the teeter-totter. But what if we substitute *fighting* for *X?* What happens if we ask kids what they *like* about fighting? Have we broken a taboo in education? Maybe, but it is for a good cause. When we do not acknowledge multiple perspectives on controversial issues, we may be guilty of pushing the party line. Students quickly get the idea that we think there is only one way to do things. Our position is too much like an embedded lecture. It is more effective when students arrive at what will work rather than the leader prompting a specific acceptable response. When students are seen as the expert on their lives, it builds on strengths, it builds resourcefulness, and it makes them more committed to the solution. If it worked so well to just tell kids what to do, we would have a bunch of angels running around in our schools! Since that has not happened yet, it seems prudent to solicit multiple student perspectives.

Case Example: Fourth Graders and Fighting

To take the previous example a bit further, imagine fourth graders talking about fighting in a group-counseling meeting. These boys all struggle with varying degrees of what might be called impulse control: They hit first, think second (OK, maybe they do not think, *yet,* but we are working on that!). In the discussion, several boys take the position that they have a right to hit because some jerk "*made me mad.*" They are full of righteousness even if they know that their position would wither in front of the steely eyes of the principal. If we ask, *Tell me what you like about hitting?* we are likely to get a barrage of "*he had it coming*" in one form or another.

Ask the unexpected. We slightly dilute the power of their position when we follow up with, *What else do you like about hitting?* This is counterintuitive, but it takes them off their routine argument and into new territory. We are doing something different. Some students will not have a second reason because they have not really ever thought about it, but we press on and repeat the question. When they run out of ideas, we might comment that we are surprised there isn't more they like about hitting since they risk so much when they make this choice. It can't be fun to miss so much recess.

After we have seeded this idea, we can ask what they do not like about hitting or, rather, the effects of hitting. Again, we pursue multiple answers by asking, *What else?* until they run out of ideas. We can cap off this conversation with, *Given all the things you have to consider, what do you think is in your best interest? He may "have it coming" as you say, but it sounds like you are the one who ends up eating it. Is it worth it to you? You seem like a very smart group; I wonder how you can outsmart the kids who try to get you all worked up. How have you been able to outsmart them in the past? What did you do?*

Does it matter if we ask what they *like* about hitting first? Or does it work as well to ask what they *do not like* first? Which order reduces defensiveness? They do not expect to be asked what they like about hitting.

Let go of the rope. When we do not try to *talk students out of something,* it is as if we are letting go of the rope in an imaginary game of tug-of-war. If no one is pulling on the other end, it ceases to be fun. When we allow students to talk about their undesirable behaviors without going into lecture mode, we let go of the rope. When we notice their strengths despite their imperfections and maintain a position of curiosity, they get to see and potentially value other sides of themselves. Once that happens, students can make choices about their behaviors and it is a whole new ballgame. Students will not always make choices that make teachers cheer, but the odds are not as stacked against them.

Take-home lesson. There is an important take-home lesson here. Do not be afraid to ask students what they like about something we wish they would magically outgrow. Give equal time to both sides of an issue. Remember, when we ask about a behavior, it does not mean we are condoning it. When we ask, it is easier for students to relinquish a defensive stance and it frees them to consider other options. The astute solution-focused leader will want to build this kind of conversation and these kinds of questions into most activities.

Attend to What May Sound Like Unrelated Ideas

Recall the SFBC assumption that complex problems do not necessarily require complex solutions. Relating this idea to the group means that students will sometimes come up with ideas that sound like complete non sequiturs to us. When we stay curious about their ideas, we can avoid any tendency to dismiss ideas that sound unrelated. Sometimes we develop a notion about how the solution *should* look. When this happens, we are not only bitten by the dreaded "should" bug, but we are also not listening *loudly*. The student may have an idea that is his or her personal skeleton key, and perhaps this unlikely solution will fit other situations. What's more, the idea that sounds unrelated to us may be exactly what prompts other students in the group to a create a workable solution.

Imagine that one of the students in a seventh-grade study skills group comes up with an idea that if he tried to smile and say hello to the teacher when he walked into the classroom each day, it might improve his reputation with the teacher. Since he is an influential member of the group, others quickly see the merits of his idea and decide to try the same approach. This social greeting may not improve their grades, but the students have learned something about what teachers like that will also help them with friendships, getting and keeping a job, and numerous other social situations. It may not be as direct as we had in mind for a student behavior that will impress teachers, but it is certainly moving in the desired direction, and it may lead to other ideas and related behaviors.

GOAL SETTING

Goal setting is an essential part of the process in SFBC groups. We are working from a solution-focused approach when the students determine the goals. Since parents and teachers commonly generate the referrals, there is some pressure to adopt their goals for students, but unless the students have developed their own goals, they are unlikely to be invested in changing anything.

Do This	Avoid This
Invite students to develop their own goals	Adopting the goals a parent or teacher has for a student
Convert goals into small, measurable steps	Setting goals that are too ambitious
Ask students to do specific ratings	Using generalities about progress on goals

Invite Students to Develop Their Own Goals

Quite often, it is possible to arrive at a goal that is student driven and that actually addresses what the teacher or parent wants as well. For example, a seventh-grade student might be referred to a group on study skills because her homework is not getting done. The parents and teacher are concerned about grades; the girl is concerned about the boy who sits two rows in front of her in math! If the leader approaches a group of students with similar homework habits on a mission to get them to agree to turn in homework, the most likely response will be a distinct lack of enthusiasm. But if the leader notes that all the group members have someone breathing down their back and asks what it is like to be under such scrutiny, the students will likely join in a conversation about how ridiculous it is to be so overmonitored. Once this agreement has been established, it is then possible to generate a conversation about what it would take to get the adults to back off, since the experience of being overmonitored is, after all, so unpleasant! The goals students develop to get the adults to back off will be remarkably similar to the goals of the parents and teachers. Students know they can get adults to back off if they do what is expected. The only difference in arriving at the same conclusion is the delivery.

Convert Goals Into Small, Measurable Steps

When we suggest that students consider experimenting with new behaviors, make it a small change. Remember the part about Rome! Students are much more likely to be successful with small changes, and success is our building block. If they fail, it is much harder to recover. If they get carried away with all they can do, hold them back; suggest that they take it slow. Help them concoct a shrunken version of a goal that is too ambitious. If they return to the group having done more than agreed to, all the better. But if they return to the group having failed, the needed repair work impedes progress.

Imagine that seventh graders in a study skills group decide that they will all get between 95 percent and 100 percent on the science quiz next week so that Mr. Johnson will see them as more than screwups. They are determined to prove him wrong. They decide to do some studying together and seem quite intent on making study guides. It all sounds great, except that none of them has ever gotten more than a C– on any previous quiz. A better goal would be something more realistic; if they exceed it, they will relish their accomplishment. Success breeds success. Following success, avoid the tendency to revise the goal upward too quickly. Continue to express amazement, but make the official goals small increments from the previous goal.

Ask Students to Do Specific Ratings

Periodically, ask students to rate on a scale of 1 to 10 (10 being high and 5 being average) where they are on their goals. Start the rating on the first day the goal is established (e.g., *Where are you now?*) and check in regularly. This provides an easy opportunity for follow-up questions such as, *What did you do to get the rating to increase?* or *How did you keep it from slipping any more than it did?* This practice helps make the goals concrete. It also reinforces even small changes. Additionally, students may have suggestions for each other on how to improve the rating next time, and these kind of suggestions are very powerful.

If ratings are done verbally, the leader will want to keep track so he or she can use comparison comments such as, *Looks like you went up on the scale. How did you get that to happen?* If ratings are done on a chart, leaders may want to keep the chart so that the record can reliably appear at the next meeting rather than become lost in the backpack with last week's tuna fish sandwich.

THE ROLE OF QUESTIONS

Questions are at the heart of the solution-focused method, and it is important to use them liberally but mindfully. It is tempting to take the activity plan that some earnest person created and published and assume that since the last activity she had was a good one, the next one will be too. We review the activity quickly and decide that it does meet our standards for an activity that is solution focused. It is not until we are halfway through the group meeting and just getting to the part about "Processing Questions" that we discover one giant flaw in our plan. The activity is textbook solution focused, but the follow-up questions are quite psychodynamic. This unnerving experience leaves us wondering what to do next. We will leave this poor, hapless leader hanging on the cliff, vowing to plan better next time, while we consider issues around follow-up questions.

Do This	Avoid This
Screen processing questions in prepared activities	Assuming the questions will work because the activity is strength based
Ask well-timed exception questions	Rushing the conversation or pushing too hard
Use questions that promote expertise	Asking *why* as it can cause defensiveness

Screen Processing Questions in Prepared Activities

Frequently, the questions recommended at the end of exercises (usually called Processing Questions) are not engaging enough. Often, these questions seem to pull for an expected or approved response. Questions such as *Did it help to talk about X?* and similar questions are leading and can feel entrapping. From an SFBC perspective, it is better to focus on something a student did well and then ask, *How did you get that to happen?* so that the "processing" is talking about strengths that become a staging area for change.

Avoid *How did you feel?* questions if you are working from a solution-focused approach. From an SFBC approach, expression of feelings is not the essential ingredient for change. Kids will tell you how they feel anyway. A preferable way of asking something similar would be, *What was it like?* or *What is your experience?* Also avoid *What did you learn?* questions. Kids find them boring in a group setting, and they make you sound like a teacher. While there is certainly nothing inherently wrong with sounding like a teacher, your role as a group leader is different. The differences in the relationship between teacher and student versus group leader and student call for a different way of interacting; this applies even if you are a teacher who is also leading a group.

Ask Well-Timed Exception Questions

Developing questions that look for exceptions becomes second nature with experience. Once the idea is firmly rooted in our consciousness, it becomes easy to see that we want to highlight what is working or has worked in the past rather than focus on the problem. For example, *What about the times you and your teacher didn't argue? What were you doing then?* The hard part is not developing the questions but rather the timing of the questions and the accompanying rationale. This is a complex concept and merits in-depth discussion.

Case Example: Middle School Madness

Let's visit a group of middle school students who are actively engaged in a conversation about "unfair" teachers. When students engage in this kind of teacher complaint, it is a fairly good bet that their behavior or attitude would be seen as problematic by teachers.

This example will examine the use of exception questions and, in more extensive discussion, move beyond that intervention to a potential resolution of the issue.

In a group meeting, the tendency is for students to one-up each other when complaining. One student's tale is usually followed by an even more explicit story of teacher injustice. With each new entry into the conversation, this inclination to hijack each others' stories is coupled with an increase in the magnitude of the indictment. When this kind of fast-moving conversation begins careening downhill, the leader may feel like a passenger on an out-of-control train. As leader panic begins to swell, we reach for the train emergency brakes—an exception question. Against our better judgment, we ask an ill-timed and poorly conceived question: *What about the teachers who are fair?* This will provoke a short stare as students look at us thinking, *Which planet are you from?*

> *"What about the teachers who are fair?"* Take a moment and consider what might be wrong with this leader question at this point. It is, after all, an exception question. Isn't that a good thing? Students need to feel *heard* before they can move beyond their rendition of the story.

Timing is everything. A simple exception question tossed out by the leader at this point will be ignored. It will seem completely out of the blue. What's needed is a transitional statement, something that will form a bridge between the *unfair* idea and the possibility that this does not describe *all* teachers. But first we may need to let the students run out of steam. Even though the conversation about "bad" teachers seems like it will never end, it will lose momentum eventually. It is at this lull in the complaining conversation that a bridging statement can be useful.

From a solution-focused perspective, we want to cooperate with students—but not necessarily agree with them. With this in mind, a bridging statement might sound like the following: *It sounds like many of you feel pretty irritated and think you have been unfairly treated. That's a hard position to be in. And it sounds like this has led to some unpleasant interactions with teachers. Even though this is a difficult situation, I am impressed by your energy, your careful analysis, and your strong sense of what you like and admire in a teacher. Since you have such a clear sense of your expectations for a good teacher, I was wondering about the teachers you have had in the past who met your expectations? Teachers who have shown you what it could be like?*

This statement ends with an embedded exception question, but it begins with an acknowledgment, empathy, compliments, and a statement about their expertise on teachers they value. The build up to the exception question forms a transition from the problem-saturated story to a potential solution. This is a crucial element in a well-conceived exception question.

I asked the exception question—now what? This conversation about unfair teachers is on the right track when students can engage in a conversation about teachers they *like*. It is fun to hear students admiring the qualities of outstanding teachers. The next step is to link this conversation to student behavior. When students admire or like a teacher, their behavior is usually better. *How do you act when you like the teacher? How would the teacher talk about you when you have a good relationship with the teacher?*

If students start bragging about how well behaved they are with teachers they like, we can count this as a moment of great fortune! We have gone from a student conversation about *"the worst teacher I ever knew"* to bravado about how well behaved they can be. It does not matter that everything they say at this point is exaggerated or perhaps embellished. We have engineered a complete reversal. We have gone

> Before you read on, how would you take a group conversation about positive student behavior and apply it to dealing with teachers with whom students do not get along?

from how bad teachers are to how cooperative students are. All that remains is to apply that exemplary student behavior to teachers they do not rate as favorably.

Handling student bravado. This is a tricky moment. There is a tendency for educators to correct students when the conversation is not a precise match with reality—and the student bravado about how well behaved they are provides a tempting moment to set the record straight. We have much to lose from casting doubt or correcting students at this particular moment. Why not let them articulate what they see as exemplary behavior and thereby increase the possibility that it will occur? As they wax eloquent about how near perfect they

> Notice how closely the question in the paragraph to the right resembles a question we typically ask following the miracle question. Students have articulated their version of a miracle, so the question appears to be a good fit. However, this question has a low probability of taking us where we want to go. Generate a rationale about why this might not work.

can be, they are creating a vision of what it will look like (just as with an answer to the miracle question). Let them get attached to the idea that they can be model students with a very specific description of their behavior. The leader is in a position to ask, *What part, even a small part, of the description of yourself could show up when you are with a teacher you do not like so much?*

Following up on exception questions. We can ask how students might apply this model behavior with more challenging teachers, but the likely response will be some variation of *"this teacher does not deserve my best,"* delivered from a moral high horse. If students give their best behavior to some-one who does not, in their opinion, deserve it, they "lose face." The issue of losing face is especially relevant in the group (vs. individual) setting. When others are watching, the dynamic is different and calls for modification. We need to come up with a better rationale.

An alternative would be to ask, *I was wondering, do you think there is much chance that you could actually influence or change your teacher?* The answer will be a fast *"No!"* It is time for another bridging statement. *Well, if you can't change your teacher, and you are the one taking a hit by getting in trouble and getting low grades, it seems like this calls for extraordinary measures. How about a small experiment? I wonder if it would make your life easier if you tried taking even a little of the brilliant approach you know works with the teachers you like, and used that same approach with the teachers you don't like so much. I wonder if it might get the teacher to back off. This is just an exper-iment. What's one small thing you could try, just as an experiment? Something that would be obvious if one of your friends was watching? And something that would prove your teacher wrong about you?*

The "wrong about you" part is the hook. This prospect is intu-itively appealing. It is also important to emphasize the *small* part of this experiment; there is a better chance for success with a small commitment. It is also important to make the chosen behavior for this experiment concrete so students can evaluate and rate something specific in the future, such as the number of times a student raised a hand in class to volunteer information or an opinion.

Epilogue. Expect that students will return to the problem story numerous times. Just because we have become "enlightened" does not mean that they will step into the pages of the book and match us with a flight into exemplary behavior. If we take on a solution-focused approach as a crusade, it is easy to get disappointed that this magic wand seems less powerful than we had imagined. But if we adopt solution-focused strategies with an appreciation that the pace of change is quite individual and we stay focused on the small steps the students make, we will arrive at what G. K. Chesterton calls gratitude—"happiness doubled by wonder." Students will amaze us.

A solution-focused inoculation is based on repeated practice with generating the wording that takes us where we want to go. Olympic gold-winning athletes envision the course as they prepare to compete. We experience the same positive effect when we practice sentences that reflect solution-focused ideas.

Use Questions That Promote Expertise

Let's return to the middle schoolers and the conversation about unfair teachers. Imagine that the group has been willing to at least list some positive behaviors that have worked in the past when getting along with teachers. It might sound like the following: *Well, I know teachers like it when you say stuff in class because they don't have to sweat about whether anyone will ever raise their hand; so when I want a teacher to like me, I try to say stuff.* At this point, questions that build on expertise could be the following:

- *How did you figure out that teachers like it when you contribute?*
- *When was the first time this occurred to you?*
- *What happened the first time you acted on this in a deliberate way?*
- *How did you make yourself raise your hand? Not all kids could have done that.*

The responses to all these questions provoke an attack of expertise. To answer any of them, students will be talking about their abilities, previously hidden or not. However, a common response will be

"*I dunno*"; the good news is that that response is perfectly acceptable. Even if students cannot come up with an answer explaining their "genius," the point has been made by the simple act of asking the question. These kinds of questions deserve follow up and repetition; sometimes students will come up with a response when they have more "think time" or after other students share their ideas. But even if students are unaware of how they solved the problem, they still retain the satisfaction of knowing the group and the leader acknowledged their expertise. The good deed has been done.

Questions That Start With *How* Make the Student the Expert

When we are seen as an expert on any situation, a bit of gratification is attached; we feel good about ourselves, perhaps a little proud, and this is a good thing. When we acknowledge that students have expert opinions about aspects of their own lives, we contribute to a self-esteem reserve. We are also tapping into an idea-factory that may not have been well cultivated to date. Students have ideas about how to solve problems, even if they are unaware of them.

Avoid Questions That Start With *Why*

Questions that start with *why* can make students defensive. They are also usually an archeological dig into the past, which is not our best move from an SFBC perspective. Sometimes questions that begin with *why* do work out well, but when in doubt, if you are new to the model, avoid *why* questions.

SUMMARY

The content of the group discussion, the students' goals, and the way we incorporate questions are essential ingredients for a successful solution-focused group. The content is related to the reason for referral, but many excellent group activities are generic and can apply to a variety of groups. In group activities, we respectfully explore the students' perspective and expertise when we inquire about both sides of an issue. As educators, our tendency is to promote the socially acceptable perspective, and this gives students ample opportunity to become defensive. In contrast, when we ask about both sides of an issue, we have *dropped the rope* in an imaginary tug-of-war and made students less self-protective.

In SFBC groups, goals are student driven because goals foisted upon them will be quickly discarded. Using ratings on a 1 to 10 scale is an effective way to track progress on goals; students find this easy to do and nonthreatening.

Questions are key to a solution-focused approach to groups. Processing questions at the end of most published activity plans merit careful review and modification as they are frequently leading or are too much like school. Exception questions require good timing and context so they do not appear to have popped out of nowhere. Questions are asked to deepen the conversation, reinforce the student, and sometimes to make a point—but no matter our intent, questions are always asked respectfully. Students may not always have an answer, and remarkably, that does not always matter.

CHAPTER SIX

From Ideas to Action

Planning and Preparation

The solution-focused ideas discussed in the previous two chapters are the basis for the actions we take in leading groups. In this chapter, we will consider the nuts and bolts of setting up a group. While the paperwork may seem mundane, it sets a tone. We establish ourselves as strength based in the way we ask for information and in the way we interact in print. There is definitely skill involved in making these routine tasks the beginning of an effective working relationship with teachers, staff, and parents. The counseling department is part of a much larger school system, and reaching out to staff and administrators early will increase your chances of success at a school.

Imagine that the principal hands you the names of the seventh- and eighth-grade students who have been repeatedly referred to the office for behavior problems. The principal asks you to see them as a group for counseling. You could follow up promptly by sending each student's parents a generic group counseling permission slip, but odds are you will regret it. The points you might get for a fast response will not compensate for a predictably poor prognosis for the students. The principal's concern about these students needs to be addressed, but grouping all the students who have behavior problems together may not be a good approach. In this chapter, we will explore the reasons for that poor prognosis by examining better ways to set up a group for counseling. Careful planning is essential to a successful group experience.

This chapter focuses on the details of getting appropriate referrals, developing a strong letter of permission, screening, deciding on group composition, scheduling magic, and creating pre- and post-evaluations. Ideas on how to increase the essential teacher and staff buy-in are woven throughout the discussion; without it we are pushing a very big rock up a very steep hill. This chapter concludes with a discussion on handling pressure and ways to work with the principal in the scenario above.

GETTING REFERRALS

Another way to do a staff survey is to list the possible group topics along with a short description of the characteristics of a student who would fit into each group. Ask the teacher to supply the names of any students who fit into each category. The description of the group helps clarify what you are looking for and jogs the memory for possible candidates. The advantage of this kind of survey is that you have both the issues and the student names with one step.

This speeded-up approach is more appropriate when you have had experience with the school and you are a known quantity. Elementary teachers may be hesitant to list the names of their students when it is your first year at the site. Until you establish yourself as someone who knows what you are doing and does it well, the protective instincts of elementary teachers may necessitate a measured process.

A common way to get referrals is to do a short presentation on group counseling along with a *needs assessment* at a school staff meeting. Near the beginning of the year, ask teachers what kinds of counseling groups they would like to see offered during the year. Some will say they do not know students well enough to comment, but others will have ideas. You might ask about schoolwide trends that have been issues in the past, such as cliques or bullying, and recommend a yearlong focus for all groups on this issue (e.g., friendship).

Another avenue for referrals is to attend grade-level meetings with teachers and discuss possible recurring issues. There may be needs that are specific to grade levels, in which case you will want to offer a variety of individualized groups. As support staff, we have credibility with teachers when we are seen as providing a service that teachers want. It is important to address identified needs. Teachers know the students best and have a perspective often deepened by years of experience. They have looked at kids as groups and are able to see trends. They are an invaluable source of information.

The trick is to get teachers involved from the start. You might use a survey such as the one shown in Figure 6.1. If you and the principal decide behind closed doors what should be offered in the way of counseling groups at your school, you may find yourself trying to schedule meetings for which no one seems to have the time. With all the mandated testing and other requirements teachers must manage, you do not want your group idea to be swept aside. You want teacher buy-in from the beginning; no brilliant idea can overcome a bad start. Keep the survey simple and short to ensure a high return. Remember that most people's favorite idea is their own, so getting teachers involved from the start is essential.

Key Features of Counseling Group Surveys

A teacher and staff survey that has a solution-focused orientation will be distinguished from other surveys in subtle ways, but the differences set the tone for other communication about students.

Teachers and Staff

Notice that the survey in Figure 6.1 is addressed to "teachers and staff." The classroom aides, playground and lunch supervisors, and the principal are all experts on the students in their charge and good sources of information. There are times when issues surface outside the classroom but never appear during instruction.

Positive or Neutral Language

The language in the survey should be respectful. Notice that most of the potential topics are listed in language that is positive or neutral. This is consistent with a solution-focused approach that emphasizes the behavior you want to see more of. However, some topic titles are more traditional (e.g., Anger Management). These issues are so ingrained in teacher vocabulary that significant modification would make it difficult for teachers and others to fill out the survey and provide useful information. Following this survey, there will be other opportunities to support a collective consciousness that represents a strength-based perception of students.

Figure 6.1

School Letterhead

Date

**Elementary Teacher and Staff
Survey on Group Counseling Needs**

It is important to offer group counseling that is relevant to the needs you see as pressing. Please take a few minutes to review the needs you see in your classroom or in the student body at large and rate the following concerns. Please add to the list if you see something in the course of your student contact that is not listed. These issues are not mutually exclusive; your opinion will help orient the groups.

	High need				Low need
	1	2	3	4	5
Anger Management	-	-	-	-	-
Bully Prevention	-	-	-	-	-
Handling Divorce	-	-	-	-	-
Foster Families	-	-	-	-	-
Friendship Skills	-	-	-	-	-
Grief and Loss	-	-	-	-	-
Managing Stress	-	-	-	-	-
Newcomer's Club	-	-	-	-	-
Peacemaking Skills	-	-	-	-	-
Self-Esteem	-	-	-	-	-
Social Problem Solving	-	-	-	-	-
Other?_____	-	-	-	-	-

Comments:

Please return to (your name)'s mailbox in the school office by (date).

Thank you.

Referrals From Teachers and Parents

Once the survey information is tabulated and you have established the theme and age level for a group, referrals can be made with a follow-up notice to teachers and parents. Letters such as the one in Figure 6.2 can lead to a deluge of referrals if they are not limited in some way. To limit the referrals to a pool you can manage, send this kind of letter to only one or two grade levels. It is important to minimize any disappointment for those who cannot be served immediately. In large schools, you could limit the distribution of this kind of letter to specific teachers, homerooms, or counselors who manage specialized school programs.

PERMISSION LETTERS

With potential candidates for a group, you are ready to draft a letter. Efforts made to draft an excellent letter to parents/guardians are well worth the time. After all, if you cannot get a permission slip signed, you do not have a group! Most important, you must get *informed consent*. The parents need to have a clear sense of exactly what it is they are signing and what giving their permission means. At the same time, you do not want to scare them away or leave them with the sickening feeling that there is something really wrong with their child.

Key Features of a Letter of Permission for Group Counseling

Parents who are reluctant to sign any permission slips or do not respond to most school requests that are out of the routine (e.g., field trips or requests for parent volunteers) may have the very kids who would benefit the most. If "no" is the typical response a parent gives, these students may be getting the least in the way of special services. Stack the odds in your favor by making your letter engaging, informative, and nonthreatening.

Walking the fine line between informed consent and being reassuring can be accomplished by drafting a letter with a few key principles in mind.

Figure 6.2

Letterhead

Date

Dear Teachers, Parents, and Guardians,

The counseling department at Valley Oak School will be offering small focus groups for fifth and sixth graders on managing stress. This could be stress caused by testing, social relationships, or any more personal issue. The group will meet weekly for a total of eight sessions, and each session will be 40 minutes long. Students will be responsible for work missed during the meetings.

Please indicate below the names of any students whom you think would benefit from being in the group. Students will be interviewed to assess interest and willingness to commit. Participation is voluntary. Parent/guardian permission will be obtained prior to beginning the group. Groups will be small, so it is likely that not all students referred will be seen immediately. However, it is hoped that all students will be scheduled sometime during the semester.

Please return this form to me in the school office as soon as possible. We plan to start groups shortly. Thank you for your recommendations.

_____

Type your name and role

My recommendations for the stress-management group:

_____   _____   _____

Parent/Guardian/Teacher name: _____

Parent/Guardian Phone: _____

Signature: _____

Parents and Guardians

Many of the students referred to you will be living with grandparents or relatives or in foster or group homes. The letter and permission slip need to be welcoming for both parents and guardians.

Primary Language

Part of informed consent means that parents must be able to read your letter. If English is the second language for the family, you may need to have the letter translated. Even when students are strong readers in English, their parents may not have the same facility. Conversational ability precedes reading ability, so the fact that you have met the parent and talked in the hall may not be enough information to make a good decision about reading ability.

Introduction

Set the letter in the context of "counseling program at our school" even if you are the whole counseling program. If you have made decisions about school needs as a school faculty, then you are operating as a "program" and can say so. For parents, there is something comforting about a student-oriented program: It diminishes the sense that their child was singled out as being in need of mental health services. This is a less problem-oriented approach.

Be Positive About Their Student

Fold in the point that all students in your groups have something to contribute. This will minimize the "there's something wrong with my kid" reaction.

Group Theme

Note the theme of your group in positive terms (e.g., How to Be the Boss of ADHD, Leadership 101, Girl Power). On the teacher and staff survey, you may have used language that was "teacher lingo," but in this letter you can use terminology that is completely strength based. You have the space for description. Explain the behaviors you will be targeting with a solution focus (e.g., peaceful resolution of conflict, ability to think before acting, how to ask for what you want in a way that increases the chance of getting it).

Specific Topics

In your letter, list topics for individual meetings, again in positive terms.

Meeting Times

Be specific about when you will meet. At the elementary level, it is best to meet at the same time or on the same day each week. At the secondary level, rotating periods minimizes the impact on any one subject area. In both cases, be clear about how missed work will be handled.

The Use of *Children*

Referring to elementary students as *children* is fine, but do not refer to secondary students that way; they hate it! They are, after all, *way* beyond crayons, even if they still have that Black Beauty lunch box tucked away in the closet! Refer to secondary students as *teens, adolescents, youth*—but never as children. Since you will be asking for their assent, they will be reading the letter.

Mandated Reporting

Decide how you will handle the issue of mandated reporting in your letter. Depending on the topic and the ages of the potential group members, your decision may vary. It needs to be addressed, but the level of detail is group dependent.

Your Phone Number

Include the office number where parents have a reasonable chance of reaching you. Calls to a school can be frustrating. You may have an office number separate from the school number or an extension that will bypass the overly detailed school phone menu. Include the days of the week and the best times to reach you. If this is not possible, let parents know specifically how and where to leave a message for you. If you have a school e-mail address, this may be preferable—but do not leave your cell or home number. This can lead to problems immediately, in the near future, or in the distant future. The generosity of your intent can easily be undercut by a parent who takes advantage of the information. Even if it is rare, it is discouraging and a problem you do not need to incur.

Your Name, Signature, and Role

At the end of the letter, include a place for your signature and be sure to type your name as well as your role at the school beneath it. If parents forget your name and need to call, they may remember to ask for the counselor, nurse, or school psychologist.

Principal Endorsement

Counselors new to the field or new to a school may find it helpful to have the principal cosign the letter of permission that goes out to parents. This is especially helpful when the principal has been assigned to the site for several years and is considered credible by parents.

What Not to Put in a Letter

Besides your personal phone number, here are some other things not to include in your letter: the names of other referred children, a comment about a specific referring teacher, or any diagnostic information. See Figure 6.3 for an example of a permission letter.

Key Features of the Permission/Signature Section

On the permission/signature section, you have a choice. You can request permission that is *active* and asks for a direct *yes* or *no* answer: "Yes, I give my permission for my student to participate" or "No, I do not give permission for my student to participate." This kind of permission is usually most appropriate at the elementary level. At the high school level, it may be appropriate to get *passive* permission. In this case, a letter goes home, but instead of asking for a *yes* or *no,* the parent returns the permission slip only if permission is *not* given for participation. Before sending out a permission letter asking for passive permission, check on school policy. Some districts routinely get permission this way, and others never use this approach.

If the group you are offering will involve the whole classroom and students will not be pulled out of a class, permission may not be necessary. Whole classroom groups may be considered part of the regular social-emotional curriculum. Again, check on school policy. A letter of information rather than permission may be sent home. In general, more information is better than less. Avoid even

Figure 6.3

Permission Letter for Elementary Parents and Guardians for
Group Counseling

Stoneridge Elementary
Counseling Department

Student: _____   Date: _____
Teacher: _____   Grade: _____

Dear Parent/Guardian,

The mission of the counseling department at Stoneridge
Elementary is to provide students with the skills needed to be successful at school and in life. Our goal is to support students in reaching their full potential. To address these goals, we offer a variety of
small counseling groups throughout the school year. We would like to
invite your child, _____, to participate in a small-group
experience on friendship. All students have something to contribute
and something to gain from this interaction with others. Some of the
topics that will be addressed are (1) what it means to be a good
friend, (2) listening skills, (3) sharing, and (4) self-control.

The group will meet for eight sessions, once a week, for 40 minutes
during the school day. The specific meeting time will be arranged
based on the teacher's recommendation. Students will be responsible for any work missed during the meetings, but teachers have
agreed to work with students to fill any gaps. The goal of the
group is to allow children to grow and learn from other students
within a small group experience.

Participation in the group is voluntary and confidential. Because
all group activities are based on a trusting relationship between
the group leader and students, all information shared is kept confidential except in certain situations in which there is an ethical
responsibility to limit confidentiality. If a student reveals information about being hurt or hurting himself/herself or another
person, confidentiality will be broken to ensure the child's safety.

If you have any questions, I may be reached at Stoneridge
Elementary on Monday, Wednesday, and Friday from 8am to 3pm at
555-4400. Please feel free to contact me for any further information.

Sincerely,

_____

Sign and type your name and role

SOURCE: Dubitsky, Macias, and Quintero (2007).

the appearance of being secretive. If you have ever been at a school when a new sex education program was introduced without parent involvement, then you know how essential it is to be transparent about curriculum decisions.

Date

You will want to know the time frame for the permission slip you have created. If you end up with too many students at one time, you may need to offer additional sections at a later date. Any slip that was signed for the previous academic year is too old, even if it is within a calendar year. Every academic year is a whole new ballgame.

Student's Name, Teacher (Elementary Level), and Grade Level

This will help you at the elementary level. You will not need to rush to the office and look up all that information when it's time to pick up students for the group.

Student Signature Line

At the secondary level, it is usually appropriate to also get students to sign the permission. Legally, they give *assent*, not *consent*. The process of having them sign a permission slip helps with commitment.

Parent/Guardian Name Printed and a Signature Line

Parents/guardians and children may not have the same last name, and you may not be able to read the signature. For this reason, include a line for the name to be printed. Should you need to make a call home, it allows you to use the correct name. Using an incorrect name can be quite awkward in situations were there has been a divorce. See Figure 6.4 for an example of a permission slip.

SETTING UP THE GROUP

Screening

Between the referral process and the first group, careful screening is in order. This is especially true when you are getting pressured to include specific students. Not all students are good candidates for a group. Some have needs far greater than a group

Figure 6.4

Permission for the Friendship Club at the Elementary Level
(Please detach and return to your child's teacher)

_____ I give permission for my child, _____, to participate in the Friendship Club.

_____ I do not give permission for my child, _____, to participate in the Friendship Club.

_____ I would like more information. Call me at _____.

_____
Parent/Guardian Name (please print)

_____   _____
Parent/Guardian Signature   Date

_____
Student's Teacher and Grade Level

can handle and may need to be seen individually. For example, some students may have specific issues that are not appropriate for a group (e.g., a history of sexual abuse that is shared too freely). These students will need individual counseling specifically designed to meet those needs with someone trained with that population. Some students may give you the distinct impression that they would take over the group and diminish others; these students might also be better served individually.

Avoid students who monopolize, dominate, or demean others. Avoid students whom you can predict will not be accepted by the group; they may feel isolated and the group could ultimately be emotionally damaging. Students who do not speak enough of the dominant language in the group may end up feeling frustrated and left out. This list of students to avoid is not complete or absolute; the intent is to offer some suggestions on the composition of the group.

Careful screening helps you avoid being in the dreaded position of having to ultimately exclude a student. Screening helps, but of course there are no guarantees. There are times when unexpected issues arise. When a student is excluded, other students may fear that they too could be excluded, even if they are relieved to have the difficult person gone.

Pressure from administrators and teachers to include specific students seems inevitable. Educators recognize a student need and want to address it, even if the "solution" is simply to get the student out of the class so the teacher can have a break. They may look to you with hope because their attempts at resolution have failed. You can make yourself unpopular pretty quickly by taking a firm stance that you will not accept a particular student in the group. Not only will you be unpopular, but you may also acquire the unflattering label of being someone who is unwilling to do the heavy lifting with the more difficult students. This puts you at risk of being dispensable.

A more effective approach involves talking it out, also known as consultation and collaboration. Explain your position and your concerns about the group. Most important, offer to do something else with the student in question. This may include seeing the student individually, making an outside referral, developing a positive behavior support plan, or making arrangements for the student to help in the lunch line or work as a cross age tutor. The point is to come up with a sensible alternative that makes it clear you are a team player and interested in addressing the needs of all students—not just the "easy kids" in a small counseling group.

Group Composition

Careful screening sets the stage for selecting group members that are complementary. The topic for group counseling will provide a certain amount of homogeneity because all students will have some relationship to the focus of the group. Having students at different levels of resolution with the topic provides heterogeneity. For example, in a group on divorce, students may be from families with a recent divorce or from families where the divorce happened a year ago. Both will have opinions on the subject, but they will be at different developmental positions. Each student will have something to offer to the others.

The ideal number of students in a group is somewhat dependent on the age level and specific issues of the students. In general, seven or eight students are a workable group and will provide enough time for members to express themselves. This number allows for some attrition while still having a solid group. However, with younger children, three to four members may be preferable. Their predictable impulsiveness and need for attention make it difficult to meet their needs and manage behavior with more than four participants. Groups should also be smaller when the referring issue (e.g., anger management) is related to behavior problems.

As the membership of the group develops, another consideration is how to strike a balance among the participants. Using the scales of justice as a metaphor, the goal is to have students who are more challenged matched with students who are less challenged (i.e., students who can function as models in some way). When we create a balance, we are building in more opportunities for students to model positive approaches for each other. Students can be very influential; hearing from a classmate about how to effectively negotiate with a new stepmother is often more powerful than anything the student's father might say. In the group, a strength-based approach means that students will have the opportunity to learn from their peers more about what works.

Avoid extremes in either direction; these students can end up feeling isolated and may drop out. Students functioning at the outside limits on the continuum may be better candidates for individual counseling. Students who have made some progress on (but have not perfected) the group topic will be able to function as a model for others. Since social-emotional development is multifaceted, it is likely that all students will function as models in some way.

At the elementary level, mixing boys and girls works well. However, at adolescence, single gender groups are preferable. The raging hormones of younger adolescents seems to make combining the genders too distracting for anything but flirting, trying to be impressive, experimenting with aggression, and being overly emotional. By high school, it may again be possible to mix the genders. This can be assessed during the screening process. There are times when a single-gender group is most appropriate no matter what the age.

Scheduling

Avoid scheduling a group during lunch at all levels. At the elementary level, avoid all recess times. Some children will insist that they do not care about recess, but we want them to care! It is a time when they mingle with peers and have to make it on their own without adults giving lots of direction. Playground survival is an important inoculation for the middle school lunchroom and rumble in the halls; they need that experience.

Scheduling groups requires patience and good negotiating skills. Teachers rightfully think that what they are doing in class is important, so deciding what to eliminate is difficult. For those schools with an after-school program, doing groups at that point can be a terrific alternative as long as transportation issues can be worked out.

Historically, the general recommendation in a letter of permission to parents has been to say something like "every effort will be made to avoid affecting academic instruction" in scheduling meetings. This promise has a high probability of backfiring. The moment you suggest to the teacher that the student miss art or PE, you will discover that the teacher was in fact an art or PE major and actually values this time above all others. A better and more strategic approach is to look to the teachers for solutions on how to schedule. They are, after all, the experts on the school day. Relying on their expertise is respectful and consistent with a solution-focused approach. Once it is their issue, there is usually more investment in making it work.

PRE- AND POSTEVALUATION SURVEYS

As support staff at a school, it is always good practice to be able to show that something we do actually makes a difference. It is not always possible to do so because some of our work is, by nature, confidential. Working with groups, however, presents a unique opportunity to gather outcome data that will guide in planning. Gathering data is consistent with good practice; it gives us the information we need to make changes and improvements. Having hard data that demonstrate the effectiveness of counseling may also help administrators fight for our jobs when there are layoffs.

Key Features of Pre- and Postevaluation Surveys

Parent, teacher, and student surveys focus on student behavior before and following the group experience. The same survey is used before and after the group meetings.

Make the Survey Topic Specific

Develop a survey that is specific to your group and that targets the behaviors the group will address. Evaluation forms can be tailored to match the goals of the group and the specific content. Questions can be continually refined or eliminated as it becomes clear which are most useful.

Analyze the Results

As counselors, many of us emphasize the practitioner side of the of the scientist-practitioner model. The thought of analyzing data may have lost its appeal long ago. However, when this hurdle is overcome, the benefits are substantial. A simple comparison of pre- and postevaluations will (1) assist with planning in the future, (2) help us improve our group material, and (3) direct us to students who may benefit from follow-up.

When the differences move in the desired direction, we can celebrate. When the differences do not go in the desired direction (and that will surely be the case some of the time), it is time to reflect, get curious, consult with others knowledgeable in the field, and avoid the temptation of blaming the students.

Figure 6.5 shows a pre- and postevaluation created for students with ADHD. It can easily be adapted for use by parents and teachers.

Figure 6.5

What's the Hype? Pre- and Postevaluation

Date: _____   Pre _____ or Post _____ Evaluation

Student Name: _____

1. I follow directions about behavior at school.
   ☐ Hardly ever   ☐ Sometimes   ☐ Most times

2. I follow directions about behavior at home.
   ☐ Hardly ever   ☐ Sometimes   ☐ Most times

3. I can find what I need in my desk and backpack quickly.
   ☐ Hardly ever   ☐ Sometimes   ☐ Most times

4. I can find what I need in my room quickly.
   ☐ Hardly ever   ☐ Sometimes   ☐ Most times

5. I finish my homework and assignments on time.
   ☐ Hardly ever   ☐ Sometimes   ☐ Most times

6. I think through what I am going to say.
   ☐ Hardly ever   ☐ Sometimes   ☐ Most times

7. I think about what to do before I do it.
   ☐ Hardly ever   ☐ Sometimes   ☐ Most times

8. I know what to do when I am mad and can avoid getting in trouble.
   ☐ Hardly ever   ☐ Sometimes   ☐ Most times

9. I have friends I like to hang out with at school.
   ☐ Hardly ever   ☐ Sometimes   ☐ Most times

10. I have friends I like to hang out with at home.
    ☐ Hardly ever   ☐ Sometimes   ☐ Most times

11. I treat my teachers with respect.
    ☐ Hardly ever   ☐ Sometimes   ☐ Most times

12. I treat my classmates with respect.
    ☐ Hardly ever   ☐ Sometimes   ☐ Most times

You're Done!! Thank you.

SOURCE: Anhar, Crisp-Handleson, Grove, and Zehnder (2006).

HANDLING PRESSURE

Let's return to the scenario from the beginning of the chapter. The principal has just handed you a list of eight students who have been recently referred to the office for discipline problems. The explicit request is that you offer these students group counseling. This is not a cheery moment. There are many reasons not to group eight students with significant behavior problems; it would be unreasonable to expect anything but bravado on how to get out of class and modeling on how to get referred to the office. However, there are obviously many reasons to work cooperatively with the principal.

The principal has unknowingly blurred the distinction between counseling and discipline. While the goal of both is change, the route to getting there is completely different. At the point at which this unwanted referral is hurtling toward you, this clearly is not the moment for a minilecture on discipline versus counseling. But this is an important issue to have worked into that staff presentation you did at the beginning of the year. When times are less heated, it is easier to see the distinction. Among many differences, discipline is imposed on the student while most counseling is voluntary. It may be possible to convert a discipline issue into a counseling referral, but it is far from automatic and takes effort.

Imagine that you *did* introduce this distinction between counseling and discipline at a staff meeting; there is no guarantee that the principal will recall it at the moment the "infamous eight" are referred for group counseling. But it will be much easier to return to that conversation if there was some general agreement made during an earlier discussion. The goal in the interaction of the moment with the principal would be to be reassuring without specifically promising anything. It might sound like, *I certainly share your concerns. It will take some planning. Let me work on this and get back to you with some suggestions in a couple of days. Can we set aside a time to meet and discuss a plan?*

After some strategizing and planning, you will be in a better position to discuss a thoughtful plan with the principal. Your goal may feel like mission impossible. You want to avoid setting up a group where all students have extreme behavior and/or attitude problems and are acting it out with enough frequency that they are getting kicked out of class. You want to avoid a big group where all students are mandated to attend. And you definitely want to avoid a group in which there is limited potential for positive modeling. But this mission-impossible group is strikingly similar to what the principal requested. There's always a way!

In the follow-up meeting with the principal, harkening back to that earlier conversation about the differences between discipline and counseling is a starting point. Don't expect applause; it may appear that you are trying to avoid the problem. It will, however, give you a framework for the problem solving that can follow. Providing a lot of explanation at this point can sound like excuses for not taking action.

A better approach is to be specific about what you propose and fold in your reasoning in small doses. You might consider offering the following:

1. Interview each of the eight students individually. Assess their interest and motivation for meeting with a group of peers to learn ways to spend less time in the office and get teachers off their back. Some may be interested. Some may be good candidates for a group.

2. As long as behaviors are not too extreme, create a group with perhaps three or four of the students and add in other students who are on their way to managing their behavior more effectively.

3. Consult with teachers and parents and develop positive-behavior support plans for the students who are not good candidates for a group.

4. Whatever plan you devise, ask the principal for input all along the way. That person is the ultimate expert on what this school needs. Even if you need to reshape the principal's ideas slightly, your goal is to stay in the ambassador role.

5. Give the principal updates along the way. You will develop influence when you are seen as a team player who is proactive. With that influence, you can be a student advocate under adverse conditions.

Creating conditions that lead to lasting change requires careful planning, and change is the whole idea—the ultimate validation that what *you* are doing is working!

SUMMARY

The mechanics of handling the paperwork to set up group counseling may seem mundane, but it sets the tone for the way we approach counseling in the schools. The attitude projected on the forms and letters we distribute influences how other professionals and parents see us. If our approach is positive, thorough, and welcoming, we will be seen as competent. Likewise, our presentation on paper influences others. When we ask about a student in ways that make room for strengths, we impact the perception that others have about a student who is challenged.

Our student surveys, letters of permission, and pre- and post-evaluation forms are carefully crafted to be consistent with a solution-focused approach. Forms and letters acknowledge the expertise of those sharing observations, request information and permissions respectfully, and highlight student strengths.

Chapter Seven

From Ideas to Action

Getting the Group Up and Running

As discussed in the last chapter, the planning and preparation involved in setting up a group help the leader get off to a good start. In this chapter, we consider how to get the group up and running, how to keep it afloat, and how to pull it together so we end well. These "how-to" action principles help align the material with a solution-focused approach and are consistent with good practice using any orientation. In the next chapter, we examine issues that can arise in the life of a group and how to troubleshoot those situations.

At the First Meeting

As you and the group members settle into the first meeting, begin by making a general statement about the purpose of the group. Leaders set the tone in the way we manage this general introduction. Take the reason for referral and tilt it toward the desired outcome; when you do this, you will have a positive way to describe why they are all sitting in the room staring at you. For example, if the fourth and fifth graders in this group were all referred because they have experienced a recent divorce in their family, you might begin by saying that the goal of the group meetings is to focus on effective ways to handle a family divorce. Since they are certainly experts on this issue, you might add that everyone here knows something about this issue and may eventually have ideas to share that will be helpful to others in the group.

Some students will know in advance exactly why they are there, or will at least think they do. A parent might have said something such as, "*I know you are upset about the divorce and it is too difficult to talk with me so I thought it would help you to get your feelings out with other kids your age; that's why I signed you up for the group the school was offering.*" This student enters the group with the expectation that it will be necessary to pour out all the gritty details whether the student wants to or not. We need to find a way to reassure this student so he or she does not flee in terror.

Other students will be completely clueless about why they are sitting there. The parents of these kids may also be worried about their children, but they may be so tied up in knots themselves that they cannot utter a word about the group to their children. The conversations in these homes are superficial and about logistics; these are the kids who are more likely to cry in bed when there is no one to comfort them. These students may be quite alarmed and even frightened sitting in the group. These students also need reassurance.

These are the two most likely scenarios; there are certainly other possibilities, but the point is that the leader has a short period of time to meet these needs by being reassuring. One way to do this is to be generally upbeat and talk with a subdued level of enthusiasm. The students will pay attention to what we say, but if we have that *do you need a tissue?* look on our face, it will set a maudlin tone. After the introductory statement, you might talk briefly about this series of nine meetings as an opportunity to get to know each other, have some fun, and learn some of the ways other kids have managed to have a good life after their parents divorced.

This is probably enough of a start before moving on to introductions. We do not want to give the impression that students will be required to be too revealing because this can be distressing. Sometimes students show up bursting to tell all; these students need to be redirected as revealing all too early often ends up as an embarrassment to the speaker after he or she finishes—it's like undressing in public. We want to prevent that and slow these students down. Additionally, when there is a student who says too much too soon, other students can feel panicky that the same will be expected of them.

Introductions

On the first day, start with activities that all students will find non-threatening. This should be something everyone can do with ease. In most groups, beginning activities will be designed to learn names and make introductions (unless you are working in a classroom group). This requires some thought; something you think is easy may not be easy for the student who has learning disabilities and cannot write or for the second-language learner who cannot easily explain the origin of his name. Students will have enough anxiety without facing an activity that makes them feel stupid or wish they had stayed home sick that day. The goal is to make it fun so that they will want to come back.

Continuing with the example of the fourth- and fifth-grade group on divorce, some of them will know each other, but given that they are from two grade levels, students are unlikely to know everyone. To learn names and get everyone to talk, make the activity simple. Students might say their name along with their favorite food, TV show, or sport. Alternatively, students might connect their name with an adjective that starts with the same letter as their name. Whatever the process, review it so that names are repeated several times and students have a chance to really learn all the names. This can be accomplished by asking, *Who thinks they can remember the names of two other students in the group?* After admiring the listening skills of the volunteer, make the task more difficult until several students can recall all the names. In this way, names will be learned as they are repeated several times. By this process, the talent of listening and remembering has been validated and established as a norm in the group, and any dread about talking about divorce has been avoided until the setting is a much safer environment.

Getting Everyone to Talk at the First Meeting

Do you remember when you were in graduate school? Can you picture a class in which you felt intimidated and reluctant to raise your hand to contribute? Once you attend several class meetings without talking, it becomes nearly impossible to cross that hurdle. The self-talk might be about looking stupid, or not knowing enough about the subject, or criticizing ourselves for not doing the reading. We often end up blaming ourselves or the teacher in our mind, but we still do not talk. The same thing happens to younger students.

At this first meeting, it is important that everyone talks. Students who leave the group without saying much may have a hard time returning. Adjusting activities to make it really easy to contribute is essential. In the name activity above, if students freeze when it is their turn for an introduction, help them out and then give a lot of thought to making room for this person in the meetings that follow.

Opening Activities: Icebreakers

Following introductions, some kind of playful icebreaker is a good fit. An icebreaker is designed to stir up the energy in the group and get the group sharing. This activity is typically short, maybe 10 minutes, and nonthreatening. Ideas for icebreakers can be found in activity books, online, and even in party game material. It does not need to be related to the theme of the group in the first few meetings. The possibilities here are endless; let's imagine that the fourth and fifth graders played a few rounds of "Have you ever . . . ?" The leader might start by giving a series of potential example questions and then begin the game with, *Have you ever climbed a tree?* The leader can do a few rounds (and demonstrate a wide variety in the content of the questions). Next the leader establishes some way for students to take turns asking the question.

Leader Always Goes First

Whenever we ask students to do something, it is good practice for us to go first. For students frozen in an anxious state, this will help thaw them out. The modeling we provide gives structure and reduces the fear some will have that responding to your request is tantamount to making a fool of themselves. When leaders demonstrate, it is also possible to show options. If you are asking the group to create an object (e.g., to work on cooperation, make a tower made of toothpicks and marshmallows), either present a model or draw one on the board. If it is not possible to have the leader demonstrate, the activity should probably be promoted to the "riskier" category and should be scheduled later in the series of meetings.

Establishing the Rules

Once students have demonstrated some ease in the group, focus the group on establishing some rules for the time together. Ask students what rules they would like to have that would make it easy to hear others and make sure that everyone feels good about being at the meeting. If you draw a blank stare from the group, you might suggest a rule by asking a question such as, *Do you think it would be good to have only one person talk at a time?*

Students often come up with rules that start with "*No,*" as in "*No put-downs*"; make an effort to get them to describe the preferred behavior and state the rule in positive terms. Limit the rules to the most important four or five, and add confidentiality if they did not arrive at it themselves. Confidentiality needs to be described in age-appropriate terms such as, *What we talk about in here is private.*

Making a poster of the rules and having all the students sign the poster works well at the elementary level. The poster can be displayed in the room. Reviewing the rules at the beginning of the next few meetings may increase compliance, but there are no guarantees! One way to review at a later meeting is to ask the following questions: *Which rule is easiest for you to follow? Which one is most difficult? What makes it so?*

At the secondary level, the process is more casual but still important. A poster is a definite no-no, but writing up a brief contract that everyone signs can have a similar effect.

Main Activity and Discussion

The level of structure of the main activity and discussion depends on both the age of the students and the specific needs of the group. In general, the younger the group, the more structure required. Think back to your history with board games and this principle will be obvious. Younger kids play games by carefully moving their token and paying close attention to their position on the board (high structure). High school kids can often ditch the board completely but are quite fascinated by the box of quiz cards and enjoy bantering and answering as a group (low structure).

The same principle applies to counseling groups. At the elementary level, our plan for each meeting is quite deliberate but always flexible as needed. At the secondary level, our plan is looser, and students have more freedom to direct the flow of the meeting. In both cases, however, we are wise to have quick alternatives ready when something flops.

With this principle in mind, we choose an activity that meets all the criteria discussed in the previous two chapters. With our fourth and fifth graders, a soft start-up is important. It may not even be necessary to discuss anything related to divorce at this first meeting. Getting them to just talk about their strengths may be a good start. *What do other people in your family say you are good at?* Notice how much easier this is to answer than to ask simply *What are you good at?* In the first case, the student is just reporting, but in the second case, the student could be accused of bragging. The goal is to eventually get to where students can outright say what they see as their strengths, but it takes some work to build up to this point.

> Think of follow-up questions for *What do others say you are good at?*

Need for Reinforcement

Start with a behavior management system in place with groups where behavior is likely to be an issue. Do not wait until you have a problem that was actually predictable from the beginning. If the behavior system is obviously not needed after you start, you can always relinquish it—but it is much harder to add it in after you are started. For example, if you are leading a group of third graders with attention-deficit-hyperactivity disorder (ADHD), it may be advisable to develop a behavioral contingency plan that includes an increase in the structure of the activities and frequent rewards. In contrast, if you are doing a group with pregnant teens, less structure and a more open format may be a better fit for reflection and problem solving. These girls may not need a token every time one of them speaks up or listens to another, but the students with ADHD might need this level of support.

Ending the Group Meeting

Some leaders find it useful to end each group with a short activity that is the same at each meeting and therefore becomes a common thread. With younger children, this could be a song and a short recap. With older students, the ending could be compliments to others in the group and maybe a special handshake. With high school students, a different question that requires a bit of self-reflection could be

> Generate a list of other questions that prompt for self-reflection.

asked with each week, such as *What did you learn about yourself today that you didn't already know? What comment today caught your attention? What was surprising?*

A review of ending activities in currently available group activity books will give the reader other ideas. These ideas will need to be judged in light of solution-focused assumptions. As you consider questions for an ending, do not ask *What did you learn today?* This kind of question puts us into teacher mode. Finally, as always, when something does not work, do something different—but we can do something different only if we are well-prepared.

End of Session One: What About Goals?

The first meeting is usually too soon to ask students to develop a goal. They need time to adjust and get comfortable; that is *our* goal for the first meeting. We seed the idea of goals indirectly when we end the first meeting by saying, *This week, notice what happens that you would like to have continue or happen more often* (adapted from LaFountain, Garner, & Eliason, 1996). By the time the group meets for a second session, they may be better equipped to focus on goals.

KEEPING THE GROUP AFLOAT

In the life cycle of many groups at the elementary level, there is a honeymoon phase in the beginning that wears off after the first few meetings. This honeymoon phase is often followed by some testing of the limits. If you have done a thorough job with establishing the group rules and have reviewed them at the beginning of each of the first three meetings, you will be able to refer back to the rules as needed: *Ah, which rule does that break? What's a good way to remember that one?*

At the middle school level, if there is a honeymoon, it will be short! In many groups, that lovely phase is skipped altogether, and you will be in *testing the limits* almost immediately. If we stumble into being too authoritative, we become a lightning rod for a challenge to our authority. A focus on student strengths right from the beginning can dilute this kind of challenge, but we do not want to abdicate our authority. We can be acknowledging without giving the group over to student leadership.

High school is another world altogether. Any honeymoon phase seems to come toward the middle and end of a successful group—after we have earned our stripes. In most groups, students will be more focused on each other and challenges to authority may be directed toward peers rather than the leader.

In keeping the group afloat, planning is critical. But the original plan we so carefully developed before we started may need a major revision after we see the group together. Beware of falling in love with the original plan because you may need to switch to plan B; if you have fallen in love, you can miss the signals that a change is what is needed.

Goals

During the second meeting, we follow up on the task from the end of session one by asking students what they *would like to have continue or happen more often* in their lives. This conversation is a version of the miracle question. With this information, we are in a position to get more concrete about goals. The setting of goals becomes the main activity for the second session.

How we ask the miracle question is important. Returning to the fourth and fifth graders who have experienced a family divorce, the more standard way of asking the miracle question may be a poor setup. If you ask a group of students about a miracle following a parental separation, many will say the miracle is having their parents back together again, something over which students have little to no control. However, we can lead into a discussion on goals by saying something like this:

> *When parents decide to get a divorce, it affects everyone in the family, not just them, and this can be uncomfortable or upsetting. Since you are all in that kind of situation right now, and since there are many things you cannot control, let's look at the parts you can do something about. What small thing that is already happening would you like to have continue or to have more of in your life?*

With this presentation, the focus is on the student—exactly where we want to be. Students may wish for things that sound irrelevant unless we are closely attuned. One student may say he wants to see his dog every day even though he is switching houses on a weekly basis and the dog lives with his mother. The fact that this boy can articulate what he finds important (and probably comforting) will help other students do a self-inventory for the same. The group can help strategize and problem solve. This student wants more time with his dog, and the group is a great venue for increasing the odds that it could happen.

While developing a miracle question in an individual session can take 20 minutes, when done in a group, the groupthink seems to spur on the discussion, with each student piggybacking on the other. It is possible to get all students to commit to an individual goal around a common theme, with other students adding to the possibilities in one session. The leader should track the specific goals in writing and refer back to them. This process can be part of an icebreaker or folded into the main activity as appropriate.

While goals are individual, students can evaluate these goals in relation to more general subject matter introduced by the leader. For example, knowing that some divorce experiences are fairly common, the leader may plan an activity that explores effective strategies for dealing with disappointment. The leader might initiate the following conversation:

We all experience disappointment in our lives. For some of us, the divorce may be a big one. Before that happened, you already knew something about how to handle disappointment. You have had to handle other bumpy situations in your lives. What do you already know about handling disappointment that might be helpful to you now? What did you do the last time you felt disappointed that helped you out or made you feel a little better? Who did you seek out to spend time with or talk to? How did you come up with that idea? How could it be useful to you now?

Look for things that are simple and practical. The ideas do not need to be earth-shattering in order to produce great results. One student may note that the last time she was pretty disappointed, she decided to start a picture journal and did a lot of drawing. She noticed that she did not think about the problem all the time and that really helped. Any students who find themselves stuck may be able to borrow an idea from a peer; this process is at the core of why groups are so important. Students can learn from each other and build on each others' ideas. It is usually a huge relief to discover that other students struggle too and that they have some interesting ideas for solving problems.

At the conclusion of the conversation on disappointment, students might do a rating on how much handling disappointment affects their individual goal (E. Macias, June 2008, personal communication). In this way, the individual goal and group discussion merge. Students might also be asked to rate (1–10) where they are now on handling disappointment and where they would like to be in a month. This information becomes secondary goals that support the primary goal. The leader can track this information.

Over time, a routine part of the group will be checking back in on goals, doing ratings, and talking about what leads to progress or setbacks. The leader may choose to have this discussion as part of or instead of an icebreaker beginning with the third session. In some groups, it is important to have an icebreaker separate from checking on goals because a good icebreaker generates energy and interest. Sometimes a quick check-in is appropriate, and sometimes a more extended discussion is a good fit.

The remainder of this section will be devoted to specific strategies that will support positive momentum as the group develops.

Create a Trajectory of Increasing Difficulty

Over the series of meetings, we can ask students to gradually do activities and have conversations that reveal more about themselves. Since it is inherently risky for most students to be self-revealing, we build these activities in slowly.

For example, let's revisit the first meeting "name game" and imagine that we add something about the preferences of the members. With younger kids, gradually increasing the difficulty about preferences may involve wording questions differently over time. For example, *Who likes ice cream?* is an easier question than *What is your favorite thing to eat?* Responding to the first question only requires an "*I do!*" or a raised hand; responding to the second question requires the student to generate an idea and then share it. What if they like something that is not very popular in the group? Students can get tongue-tied over worries that their idea will be rejected.

In a group for younger kids who are shy and struggling to speak up, we might start with questions phrased so that little verbalization is required to participate initially; with success at that level, we can increase the difficulty—even within the same meeting.

> If we were to make a list of types of questions from easy to difficult, what question would be intermediate between the two listed above? One possibility is a forced-choice example such as, *Which do you like better: ice cream or pizza?*

With secondary students at the initial gathering, we might ask them to pick an adjective that starts with the same letter as their name and ask them to use that adjective when introducing themselves. They are in control of the word that describes them, and they can choose to be funny, serious, goofy, or intellectual. This makes the activity less threatening for most students. We may get *Lucky Larry, Sexy Susie, Awesome Alouise, Brilliant Brian.* It is easier to recall the names with a moniker attached, and being called by name is extremely important. We want students to feel seen and known from the beginning. This fosters belonging and boosts self-confidence.

> To ensure ease with the name task, what might the leader do in advance of asking students to create adjectives? What if one student freezes when it is his or her turn? Read on after you have some ideas. In the first case, the leader might run through a list of possible adjectives as a brainstorming activity prior to starting. In the second case, the leader might say, *As Mary reviews some possibilities in her head, let's give her some ideas that start with M.* And how will you help Xavier and Yelena? Planning is everything! Come with ideas.

The issue of creating a trajectory of increasing difficulty is more complex than it may appear at first glance. Start with activities that do not require much revealing of self. Gradually increase the required level of self-exposure while giving students choices over how much they are comfortable revealing.

This approach is sensible but not always so easy to accomplish. In the example of a group on divorce, students may find it relatively comfortable to talk about *stepparent syndrome* and ways to form an effective relationship with the new person. This conversation is based on a typical concern and related to loyalty to parents.

However, not everyone in the group may feel the same way. It may be much harder for the students who are sitting there thinking that they prefer the *new* person to their mother; the new person is less stressed, pays attention to the kids, and is funny. Students can feel quite conflicted and upset about these kinds of observations. Just when it seemed that we had structured activities so that we began with less revealing material, we may find ourselves surprised by a student's distress; we need to be prepared to include that person.

Harkening back to the idea of giving attention to multiple perspectives on the same issue (both sides of the teeter-totter), we might simply say, S*ome of you may be finding it difficult to deal with your new stepparent. Changes like this take time. It may also be the case that some of you are actually relieved that the fighting at night has stopped and that the new person makes you laugh or pays attention to you. That might make for some mixed feelings.* This kind of comment makes a space for that student to say something if she or he wishes to. Asking students a direct question, however, may be asking them to reveal more than they can manage. This may amount to increasing the difficulty too quickly and can be frightening, leaving the student too exposed. Better to create the opening, pause, and then move on. The students now know that their feelings are an acceptable topic, so they may resurface at a later date.

How Much Action-Based Activity Is Appropriate?

Some group activities call for a good deal of movement. This is particularly true of activities that come from the outdoor education or ropes course tradition. These activities can be very thought provoking, and they develop team bonding by engaging in shared tasks and problem solving. These kinds of action-based adventure activities have a place in school counseling groups as long as some thought is given to several issues. First, what is the goal of the activity? In the early stages of the group, the general goal is to build trust and camaraderie. Action-based activities can be a good fit here, especially if subgroups or pairs work together to accomplish something. But if the activity will result in a lot of running around and the classroom next door is doing silent reading, the group will not be a popular idea with that teacher. In addition, even if the activity is spectacular, if it will get a group of third-grade boys who have ADHD all worked up, it is likely to be counterproductive. Their teachers will not appreciate having them return to the classroom all wound up, so the effects and aftereffects of the activity merit consideration.

Successful Ways to End a Group

Students need to prepare for ending a group a couple of meetings before the last gathering. While students may have known at some point that there would be eight or nine sessions, they are unlikely to track the weeks. Avoid having the last meeting come as a surprise. Advance notice gives any students wishing to talk about something (but who are reluctant to do so) a chance to gather their resources. If students are enjoying the group, they will feel a loss with its ending. Sometimes there is a lobbying effort to extend the timeline; the leader may want to consider how to respond to this request before it erupts.

Ending any solution-focused group involves some wrap-up activities that are geared toward bringing closure to the series and setting in motion future change.

Review Initial Goals and Progress to Date

While goals have been reviewed all along during the meetings, the final meeting is an opportunity to highlight progress, get curious about how progress was made, celebrate successes, and strategize about any roadblocks. If we ask, *Are you surprised that you made as much progress as you did?* it is important to also ask, *Are any of you surprised you didn't make more progress? What will it take to get just a little closer to your goal?* If a student appears stuck, it may be time to revise the goal, even if it was revised earlier.

Make Plans to Keep Moving Toward Goals

Some students will have reached their goal, and others will not have. Students who have reached their goal may want to sketch out any next goals. Students who are still in process will need encouragement to keep going. The conversation continues to be based on student expertise: *What will it take for you to keep going on something that's important to you and maybe not so easy? What will be a marker for you that you are making progress? What will you be telling yourself that will keep you on track? Who will be happy for you, maybe even surprised when you make progress?*

Predict a Relapse and Strategize for a Comeback

Since progress for most of us is uneven, a good way to prepare students for some backsliding is to predict a relapse. If the predicted relapse does not happen, no harm done. But if students find themselves back at the starting gate, it helps to have been forewarned and to have a plan for digging out. Predicting a relapse normalizes the possibility. Since the normalizing conversation takes place in a group, students may be able to support each other during a relapse and offer reassurance long after the group is over. Predicting a relapse is like an inoculation for success.

Pick the Support Team

When reviewing goals, include a conversation about who is likely to cheer them on. Get specific. The support team may have some unusual members, including pets. We might ask how someone on the team is supportive, but it is important not to disagree. Support may materialize in mysterious ways.

Share Compliments

Activities at the last meeting should include some way for students to give compliments to each other. There are many options for this. The leader may give compliments, too, especially with younger students, but at the secondary level, the peer support is the powerhouse.

With younger students, some training on what constitutes a compliment may be in order, but do not be surprised if they get stuck on *I like your shirt!* You might ask, *What else do you like about Jeremy?* but the shirt part is actually pretty important at the first-grade level.

At the secondary level and with younger groups with good writing skills, the compliment activity can be combined with creating something students will take with them once the group is over. Having a sheet with each student's name at the top and passing the sheet around the group so that each member writes on each sheet nets a handy list of compliments. Some students have been known to save these pages for years.

Several years ago, there was a story that floated around the Internet (author unknown). The story will be adapted here from memory. It was about a young man who had died in a tragic accident. As his parents prepared for his funeral service, they went through his belongings and papers looking for pictures and other mementos that might comfort them. They came across a list of compliments prepared by classmates when he was a boy . . . something he had saved from his younger days. The family was deeply touched by this kind list and decided to read the compliments at his service.

Classmates were moved as they listened attentively to the description of their friend as seen through the young eyes of his schoolmates. At the conclusion of this reading, something remarkable happened. One woman reached into her purse and came up with a similar list, one she had always carried with her. A man reached into his wallet and produced a shredded, water stained piece of paper from the same class exercise. Others commented that they knew exactly where their paper was—carefully pressed into the pages of a yearbook. Those compliments and having something concrete had a significant impact.

Ask for Volunteer Consultants for Future Students

One way to continue to build on student expertise is to ask participants if anyone would be willing to be consultants to other students who face challenges similar to their own. Once the group is over, the counselor may have the opportunity to link a former group member with a fellow student (who is the same age or younger) to share thoughts on how to manage their mutual challenge. Most students greet this possibility with measured ecstasy! The *measured* part is related to needing to be cool, and being too enthusiastic breaks the cool sound barrier. The *ecstasy* part is connected to the immense pleasure most will take at being seen in such an official way as an expert.

When a student consults with a peer, it may work best to have both students join the counselor while the counselor does what amounts to an interview with the expert. Younger students are usually dazzled by this and the expert does emotional cartwheels all the way back to class when it is over!

Give Certificates or Letters of Appreciation

At the conclusion of the meeting, hand out certificates with each student's name carefully printed and a specific compliment written on each one. If you find certificates corny, reconsider. At the elementary level, it should be routine to have them available for all. Some students at the secondary level may find them too childish if they do, in fact, look childish; this is one more time where creating something that is developmentally appropriate really matters. As adults, we still get certificates, licenses, and awards; some of us frame and post our awards on our office walls. Not all students will cozy up to this idea; some certificates will be forgotten when they leave the room. But for many students it is one more way we can say *You are valued,* and it is such an easy way to do something that important.

Postsession Evaluations

If you did presession evaluations, you will want to complete the process with a postsession evaluation. Sometimes we get most of the information we need from the ratings of goals, but pre- and postevaluations are a helpful way to demonstrate that something really happened, even if the ratings are not all positive.

Epilogue

The most important question to ask ourselves as we review the experience is, *What changed as a result of spending this time together as a group?* Some of the change set in motion will need time to percolate, but we likely have some idea about what looks promising. Track changes over time by casually greeting kids and inquiring when you pass them in the halls, but do so privately so that confidentially and confidence in you is not breached.

We sometimes exhale loudly when the group is over, because there certainly is pressure involved in leading groups, making the time to do it, and staying prepared. But if you notice yourself missing the students when the next week rolls around and there is no meeting scheduled, you will not be alone. While it takes effort to lead groups well, the rewards are many. Students will amaze us, and as we continually get better at leading solution-focused groups, we will amaze ourselves.

One of the intriguing parts about leading counseling groups in schools is the opportunity for the leader to continue to stretch and deepen professionally. Each group is a chance to learn something new. It is possible to lead groups by whipping out a prepared group curriculum and following it much like the novice cook adheres to a recipe. But this approach will backfire eventually because the leader will be unprepared for the unexpected. The trouble with students is that they do not know they are supposed to be inert ingredients. They are active, unpredictable, and captivating—and the ideas, behaviors, and feelings they share warrant a flexible and responsive approach.

SUMMARY

This chapter covers a variety of complex issues that leaders will need to ponder and act on in order to be successful with students in counseling groups. The first meeting is a world unto itself and requires special planning. Once launched, the group plan may need to be revised based on ongoing assessment. Ending the whole series of meetings presents an opportunity to review goals and make a plan for the future. The leader can consider what the students might take with them to remind them of the experience.

CHAPTER EIGHT

Group Agendas

A Sampling

In this chapter, the ideas and action principles of solution-focused brief counseling (SFBC) are applied to actual group agendas. The nine group agendas in this series are separated by age and theme. The first three meetings are for third graders; the topic is developing friendship skills. The reader will have an opportunity to see how you might start a meeting, introduce the topic, develop guidelines, and establish an ending activity with younger elementary students. Notice how individual goals are woven into a more general discussion each week.

The next three agendas on peer pressure were developed for middle school students. The group is called Holding Your Own. The agendas are for meetings four through six out of a nine-meeting series. In this situation, a group goal of *standing up to peer pressure* was established prior to the fourth meeting. Individuals then created a more specific personal goal that was consistent with the larger goal. The discussion of personal goals is woven into a more general discussion each week.

The final three agendas are for a high school group. The topic is *decision making and setting life goals*. The author created some interesting ways to do ratings with an activity flair. The reader has the opportunity to see how one might end a whole series of meetings. The students leave the group experience with something concrete to remind them about their strengths.

These agendas were developed by graduate students at California State University, Sacramento, in the School Psychology Program in 2008: Gabriela Macias, Marianne Dubitsky, and Cynthia Quintero. Each unit has a primary author noted with the material. The final product is based on collaboration among all authors and Leslie Cooley.

ELEMENTARY LEVEL: MAKING FRIENDS

Sessions 1 Through 3

Gabriela Macias

FRIENDSHIP CLUB

Session 1

Introductions

Meeting Objective

Students will get to know each another and establish group guidelines.

Opening Statement

The goal of our time together is to learn how to use our strengths so that we can keep and make happy friendships. Also, we will learn from each other what works best in keeping good friendships.

Icebreaker: A Tangled Web

Materials needed:

Large yarn ball

1. The group leader and the students sit in a circle on the floor.

2. While holding the yarn ball, share the following instructions:

   We are going to play a game that will help us in getting to know each other a little bit better by getting to know our names and one thing that you like in your friends. First, once you have the yarn ball in your hands, share your name and one thing that you like in your friends. Then, you are to toss the yarn ball to someone in the group sitting across from you who hasn't shared, but you must keep holding on to your piece of yarn. As everyone shares, try to remember as many names as you can and, if you're up for the challenge, try to remember what they like in their friends. After we're done sharing, we will have created a "tangled web"!

3. The group leader starts.

4. Make sure everyone gets a chance to share.

5. After all students have shared, the group leader volunteers to be the first to recall the names and qualities in friends that the students shared (this will also give students a second chance to hear and remember names).

6. Ask, *Who thinks they can remember the names of two students in the group?* After admiring the listening skills of the volunteer, make the task increasingly difficult until a few students can recall all the names.

7. Have all the students stand up as they continue to hold on to the yarn. Admire the web!

8. End with a statement about the web and its relation to teamwork and friendships.

Establishing Group Guidelines

Materials needed:

Large poster board
Markers

1. Share with the students that, as a group, they will develop a few group guidelines.

2. Ask, *What guidelines would be beneficial so that everyone has an opportunity to share and be heard?* (see the list that follows for a few group guideline ideas).

3. As students come up with guidelines, make sure to phrase these in positive terms.

4. Limit guidelines to about four or five and write them down on the poster board.

5. Have students commit to the guidelines by signing their names on the poster board.

6. Laminate the guidelines poster board and post it in the gathering room.

Possible Group Guidelines

1. Always raise your hand before speaking.

2. Be respectful to everyone around you, including yourself.

3. Listen carefully when someone else speaks.

4. Use polite words, even when you're upset.

5. Keep your hands and feet close to yourself and in your space.

6. Laugh *with* your friends.

7. What we talk about in our meetings is private (include if students do not add it).

Compliment Cards

Materials needed:

Index cards
Fine-tip markers
Decorative stickers
Compliment card decorative carrying bag

Activity

1. Share with students that the name cards they will be creating next will be used at the end of every session as part of a closing ritual. The name cards are part of a compliment activity that will be explained when they are finished making a decorated card with their name on it.

2. Pass out an index card to each student, and have students write their name and decorate the index cards with markers and stickers. The group leader should also participate in the activity.

3. Allow students to chat with each other, fostering group cohesiveness.

4. Once everyone has completed the activity, collect the compliment cards and place them in the carrying bag.

Discussion

Engage in a discussion regarding the importance of friendships. Ask, *How are friendships important to you? Think of a time when a friend did something that was very meaningful to you. What happened? There are many ways to be a good friend to others. What is the way you like to be a friend? What do you do? Can people in your family be your friend too? Can a pet be your friend?*

Homework prompt: *Think about someone whom you see regularly, maybe one of your neighbors or a family member whom you think is a good friend. Over the next week, you will be observing that person (without telling them) to see what it is they do that makes them such a good friend. Check out how they act that makes them a good friend. Next week you'll be able to tell us what you noticed.*

Ending

To summarize, ask, *Who can remember one group member's name or one friend quality shared during the tangled web?*

Closing Ritual: Compliment cards created by students

Provide students with a few examples of friendly compliments. They will then randomly select an index card with a name written on it from a bag. Tell them, *You are to compliment the person whose name is on the card. Everyone in the group will give and receive a nice compliment!*

Each week, group members will randomly select a name card and compliment that person.

FRIENDSHIP CLUB

Session 2

Friendship Goals

Meeting Objective

Students will identify a friendship goal.

Icebreaker

1. Ask, *Who thinks they can remember the names of two students in the group?* After admiring the listening skills and memory of the volunteer, make the task increasingly difficult until a few students can recall all the names.

2. Review the group guidelines.

Friendship Goals

Materials needed:

Friendship Goal Worksheet
Pencils and erasers

Activity

1. Have students reflect on the homework prompt from the previous session. *Remember you were going to observe someone you thought was a good friend. Who can share with the group something they saw the person do that seemed like a good way to be a friend?*

2. Ask students to share with the group the behaviors they observed.

   Search for strengths. *What are some things you've done in the past when making friends? How did you do that?* Using a "curious" approach, ask questions that highlight students' strengths (e.g., *Wow, that is very impressive, would you mind telling us how you did that?*).

3. Ask the miracle question. *Suppose that while you were sleeping, a miracle happened. The next day when you went to school, you suddenly noticed that making friends was super easy. What would have changed in your morning that would let you know a miracle happened? What would you be doing that you are not doing now?* Give students 1 to 2 minutes to think about it and respond. If they are having difficulties coming up with something, say *If everything was perfect today, how would making friends be easier for you?*

4. Engage in discussion. For students who are comfortable, allow them to share their miracle. As they share, search for strengths and exceptions and highlight these to the group. As the discussion progresses, point out that each student's miracle is his or her friendship goal.

5. Provide students with a Friendship Goal Worksheet and have them write their responses in the appropriate section.

Ending

Summarize the session.

Closing Ritual: Compliment cards created by students

Using the name index cards, have group members randomly select a card and compliment that person.

FRIENDSHIP CLUB

Session 3

Sharing With Friends

Meeting Objective

Students will relate sharing to their friendship goal.

Sharing With Friends

Materials needed:

White paper
Fine-tip markers and/or colored pencils
Friendship Goal Worksheet

Activity

1. Ask, *Last week we talked about friendship goals. Who remembers what their goal was?* Pass out students' Friendship Goal Worksheets. Invite students to keep their personal goal in mind as the group discusses a general friendship topic.

2. Ask, *What do you think about "sharing"?* Explore both sides of the issue.
   a. *Has anyone ever shared something with someone?*
   b. *How did you do it?*
   c. *What was that like?*
   d. *What about a time you didn't share with someone? What was that like?*
   e. *What are some things you share with others? Anything you don't share?*
   f. *Is sharing helpful to you or your friends? Is it ever hurtful?*

   Allow students to discuss; when appropriate, search for exceptions!

3. Give students one sheet of white paper (if developmentally appropriate, the group leader may choose to engage in a group discussion of the following prompt).

4. On one side of the white paper, instruct students to draw a picture depicting a time when they shared something with someone even though it was difficult to do so and, in the end, felt good about doing it.

5. On the other side, instruct students to draw a picture depicting a time when they didn't share but had a feeling they should have.

6. Ask, *Would someone like to share their drawing?*

7. Engage in discussion. *What's it like when someone shares with you? What's it like when they don't? How does sharing affect your friendships?*

8. Have students track their friendship goal by filling out the appropriate section on the Friendship Goal Worksheet. Note any changes and inquire how they got that change to happen.

Ending

To summarize, ask, *On a scale of 1 to 5, 1 being "very little" and 5 being "very much," does sharing affect your friendship goal? Show me with your fingers.* Acknowledge responses.

Closing Ritual: Compliment cards created by students

Using name index cards, have group members randomly select a card and compliment that person.

Name: _____

FRIENDSHIP GOAL WORKSHEET

I would know a miracle happened if

_____

_____

_____

_____

This is my friendship goal.

Tracking my Friendship Goal

1	2	3	4	5
No Progress	Little Progress	Okay Progress	Good Progress	Very Good Progress

Session 3, Date: _____

This week I achieved ____ toward my Friendship Goal.

Session 4, Date: _____

This week I achieved ____ toward my Friendship Goal.

Session 5, Date: _____

This week I achieved ____ toward my Friendship Goal.

Final Session, Date: _____

By participating in the *Friendships,* I achieved ____ toward my Friendship Goal.

MIDDLE SCHOOL: HANDLING PEER PRESSURE

Sessions 4 Through 6

Marianne Dubitsky

HOLDING YOUR OWN

Session 4

Pros Versus Cons

Meeting Objectives

Group members will be able to identify the pros and cons of peer pressure situations.

Group members will use common peer pressure situations to practice reasoning and decision-making skills.

Guess the Object

Materials needed:

One piece of poster paper for each situation and markers.

Activity

Preparation: Create a list of common peer pressure situations that arise during middle school years, such as stealing, cheating, or vandalizing property.

1. Ask the group members to review their personal goals agreed upon from previous sessions. Invite students to keep their personal goal in mind as the group discusses general peer pressure issues.

2. Brainstorm common peer pressure situations. Give examples from the previous week if necessary. Ask the group members to summarize the pros and cons of peer pressure as discussed in previous sessions.

3. Choose one situation to review. Write the situation on the top of the poster paper. Draw a T-chart underneath with pros on one side and cons on the other. (The leader may wish to record student responses if the group is not able to focus during the discussion of pros and cons.)

4. Ask group members for one pro of the situation and one con. Alternate pros and cons in discussion until the group members run out of ideas.

5. Divide group members into pairs (or allow them to choose a partner). Give each pair a different situation (or allow them to choose) and a piece of poster paper. Ask the pairs to write down pros and cons for their situation. Group member pairs may choose to brainstorm ideas together or take sides representing either the pro or the con.

6. Give each pair an opportunity to share their pros and cons with the larger group.

7. Give the rest of the group an opportunity to add pros or cons to each pair's list.

Discussion

Rank the pros and cons from each situation from least to greatest. Choose the greatest pro and greatest con for each situation. Discuss that pro versus that con. Discuss what that pro or con would mean for a person's future. Ask, *How will you know you've made the decision that is right for you? What will tell you?*

Ending

Summarize the session. Ask students about pros or cons in relation to their personal goal. Introduce a new closing activity.

Learning to Express an Opinion

Each week, the group will end with the opportunity for each group member to share an opinion with which others may disagree. This provides group members with an opportunity to be assertive when expressing their own ideas and disagree without making someone angry. Each week's question will increase the level of disclosure; in later sessions, time for rebuttals may be appropriate.

Present the group with a question. Ask group members to share their preferences and their reasoning. The leader will be the first to respond.

Question: *What is your favorite food and why?*

HOLDING YOUR OWN

Session 5

Alternative Detectives

Meeting Objectives

Group members will be able to identify motivations behind resisting peer pressure.

Group members will learn to find alternatives to peer pressure.

Guess the Object

Materials needed:

One piece of poster paper for each situation and markers.

Activity

Preparation: Review common peer pressure situations that arise during middle school years such as stealing, cheating, or vandalizing property.

1. Ask the group members to do a self-rating on their goals agreed upon from previous sessions. Ask about any changes in ratings and any thoughts about how the ratings changed. Invite students to keep their personal goal in mind as the group discusses general peer pressure issues.

2. Reintroduce common peer pressure situations that have been used in previous sessions. (Review the pros and cons of those situations if they have already been recorded.)

3. Choose one situation to use as an example. Remind the group that there are pros and cons to every situation. Explain to the group that they will be playing detectives to figure out how some people resist peer pressure situations, how some people give in to the pressure, and what makes it hard to resist. Ask the group to brainstorm what a person may get from engaging in that situation (i.e., what are the pros of that situation?).

4. After the pros have been listed, tell the group that there are other ways to get those feelings or rewards. Ask the group members to list alternative ways of getting those results without giving in to that peer pressure situation. (e.g., If the pro is "getting people to like you," an alternative may be to join a team or club where friends can be made.) Ask, *How do you get the same results without getting in trouble? What are other possibilities?*

5. Divide the group members into pairs (or allow them to choose a partner). Give each pair a different situation (or allow them to choose) and a piece of poster paper. Ask each pair to brainstorm pros of their situation and other ways to achieve those rewards. (Alternative: if students have previously recorded pros of peer pressure situations, those pros may be used instead of brainstorming new ones.)

6. Give each pair an opportunity to share their pros and alternative activities with the rest of the group.

7. Give the other group members an opportunity to add alternative activities to each pair's situation.

Discussion

Choose one pro and paired alternative from each situation. Discuss which activity has the best chance of a positive outcome, the peer pressure situation or the alternative situation. Discuss which activity is better for the person in the long run. Ask, *How do you know which activity is better in the long run? What from your experience leads you to that decision? Discuss how to recognize alternatives in real life situations. How do you figure out what to do when you are stuck?*

Ending

Summarize the session. Ask students to think about their personal goal and share any alternatives they may have considered that could be helpful in reaching their goal.

Learning to Express an Opinion

Each week, the group will end with the opportunity for each group member to share an opinion with which others may disagree. This provides group members with an opportunity to be assertive when expressing their own ideas and disagree without making someone angry. Each week's question will increase the level of disclosure; in later sessions, time for rebuttals may be appropriate.

Present the group with a question. Ask group members to share their preference and their reasoning. The leader goes first.

Question: *What is your favorite kind of music and why?*

HOLDING YOUR OWN

Session 6

Bag of Tricks

Meeting Objectives

Group members will develop appropriate responses to combat peer pressure situations.

Group members will learn to use those responses in peer pressure situations.

Guess the Object

Materials needed:

Small strips of paper and pencils
Small paper bag

Activity

Preparation: Review common situations that arise during middle school years that have been used in previous sessions.

1. Ask the group members to do a self-rating on their goals agreed upon from previous sessions. Invite students to keep their personal goal in mind as the group discusses general peer pressure issues.

2. Ask the group for one example of a peer pressure situation discussed in a previous session. Tell the group that there are many ways to respond to that situation (e.g., stealing something from a convenience store—someone tells you to grab a couple sodas while he or she distracts the cashier).

3. Give each group member two or three small strips of paper. Ask each group member to record at least one possible response to the example situation. (Alternatively, if writing will pose a problem, the leader may need to supply all the potential responses on strips of paper.)

4. Ask group members to place their responses in the paper bag. It might be necessary to add a few responses from the group leader to ensure anonymity or add to the amount of possible responses in the bag.

5. Read aloud each response to the group and discuss how it can be used with the peer pressure situation. Ask students to categorize responses as either "giving in to peer pressure" or "resisting peer pressure." Place all

responses judged as "resisting pressure" back in the paper bag labeled "Bag of Tricks."

6. Divide the group members into pairs (or allow them to choose a partner). Give each pair a different situation (or allow them to choose) and ask them to role-play the situation, with one person as the one creating peer pressure in the situation and the other student resisting the pressure. Group members may use responses thought of on their own, remembered from the activity, or may choose blindly from the bag of tricks.

7. After a few minutes of role playing, ask the group members to switch roles, using the same situation. Group members may use responses thought of on their own, remembered from the activity, or may choose blindly from the bag of tricks.

Discussion

Ask the group to reflect on the role playing situations. Discuss which parts were easy and which parts were more challenging. Discuss ways of carrying a bag of tricks to combat real-life peer pressure situations. Ask, *How have you found ways of carrying a bag of tricks in real-life situations? What can you do to fill your bag of tricks with powerful responses?*

Ending

Summarize the session. Ask students how having a bag of tricks will effect their personal goal.

Learning to Express an Opinion

Present the group with a question. Ask each group member to share their preference and their reasoning.

Question: *What is your favorite video game and why?*

HIGH SCHOOL: MAKING DECISIONS AND LIFE GOALS

Sessions 7 Through 9

Cynthia Quintero

EXCEL!

Session 7

Looking Ahead

Meeting Objectives

Students will identify long-term goals.
Students will identify personal qualities and interests.

Activity: Looking Ahead

Materials needed: None

1. Review previous session on short-term goals.

2. **Note: For the following activity, pause after each statement and question to allow for process.** Introduce the activity Visualizing My Future by asking students to take a journey into their future. Invite students to close their eyes.
   Proceed by saying,

   Imagine yourself stepping forward into a time five years from now. How old will you be? Create a picture of where you want to be with as much detail as possible. What are you doing? What would be different in your life? Now, visualize yourself stepping forward into another time. You are now in a time that is ten years from now. Create a picture of where you want to be with as much detail as possible. What are you doing? What would be different in your life? As you prepare to return to the present, make a mental note of what you've seen and how you would like things to be. You may now open your eyes.

3. Invite students to share their experience.

Discussion

Ask, *What did you like about where you were in five years? ten years?*
   From this experience, what would you say your goal is in five years? ten years?

What qualities do you see in yourself that will help you achieve these goals?

What qualities might get in your way? How will you deal with any qualities that may slow you down?

What leads you to believe this is a good match with your future goal(s)?

What do you need to get you there?

What is already happening that you could use to begin moving toward your goal?

Ending

Allow students to review their long-term goals.

Ask, *How could you begin achieving your five-year goal on a very small scale for the next week?*

Final thought: *What surprised you most about your future?*

Remind students of the time of next week's meeting if sessions are on a rotating schedule.

Note to leader: At the end of the meeting, jot down the five- and ten-year goals for each student as they will be used in future sessions. You may need to refer to these notes if students forget.

Excel!

Session 8

Success—What Does It Take?

Meeting Objectives

Students will identify qualities for success.
Students will identify strategies to overcome challenges.

Energizer: How's It Going?

Materials needed:

Ten 8 1/2 × 11 sheets of paper, numbered 1 to 10
Tape
Setup: Post numbered paper around the room in consecutive order: 1 to 10.
Review previous meeting on long-term goals.

Ask students to go back in memory to last week and retrieve their five-year goal. Ask them to think about *small steps* and talk about any action they took during the week toward that goal.

Proceed by saying,

On a scale of 1 to 10, with 1 being "no progress" to 10 being "excellent progress," where are you today? Stand by the number that best represents your progress.

Ask, *What makes you a "#" today? What have you done that moves you in the direction you want to go? What small steps have you taken, even if it doesn't seem so closely related?*

Ask, *Where do you want to be when you come back next week?* (Ask students to move to that number.)

What will you need to do to move up on the scale?
How will you do this?
What is already happening now that you could use to help you?
Students return to their seats after discussion.

Success—What Does It Take?

Materials needed:

Six 3 × 5 index cards per student
Markers

Activity

1. Introduce the topic by asking students to take a trip down memory lane, beginning with elementary school. Give each student six index cards. They will use two cards at each school level.

2. Ask each student to think of a time when she or he successfully overcame a challenge in elementary school (could be school or family related). Write the challenge on one card and the qualities that made them successful on a separate index card.

3. Continue the activity by asking for examples in junior high and high school, allowing students to write challenges and the qualities that made them successful on separate cards.

4. Invite students to look over all the qualities that helped them be successful.

Discussion

1. *What qualities do you possess that have helped you overcome challenges in your life?*

2. *Are the qualities from elementary school times as powerful now as they were when you were younger?*

3. *What about the success qualities from middle school?*

4. *What has having these qualities allowed you to do that you might not have been able to do without them?*

5. *How did you manage to become successful despite the challenges you faced?*

6. *Of the qualities you've listed, which ones did you rely on most?*

7. *Which qualities would you like to strengthen?*

8. *How would you do that? What would be different?*

Ending

Express curiosity about how students will use their qualities in moving up the scale toward their five-year goals. Collect all cards, sort by name, and save for next session.

Final thought: *What did you learn about yourself today that you didn't already know?*

Remind students of the time of next week's meeting if sessions are on a rotating schedule. Also remind students that next week is the last session.

Excel!

Session 9

Seize Your Power!

Meeting Objectives

Students will incorporate short- and long-term goals.
Students will identify a support system.

Seize Your Power

Materials needed:

Numbered posters from previous session displayed around the room.
Index cards from previous session.

Activity

1. Review the previous meeting on qualities that make you successful. Ask students to reflect on any small step they have taken toward their five-year goal, even if the good outcome was an accident or luck! Rate their progress on a scale from 1 to 10, with 1 being "no progress" to 10 being "excellent progress." If a student made progress on the scale, ask *How did you manage to move ahead? What did you do? What affect does that have on you?* If a student stayed the same, ask *How did you manage to stay the same or not move backward?*

2. If a student moved backward, there are several possibilities for questions; the decision on which question(s) to use depends on the student, their resources and attitude. Some of the following questions may be helpful, and others may not be so useful. *What's it like for you to shift back on the scale? Are you aware of anything that contributed to that outcome? Are there things that are outside your control that contribute to this outcome? Does this seem like an OK place to be right now? If you want to move up on the rating, what do you need to do to make that happen? Is there anyone who might be helpful to you to move up on the scale?*

3. Discuss with students that the small step they have been working on toward their five-year goal is also known as a short-term goal (covered in a previous session).

4. Ask, *When you have accomplished your current short-term goal, what do you believe should be your next step? What will you need to get there?*

5. Say, *Sometimes setbacks can happen as you work toward a goal. Don't panic! Look at what you need to move ahead. Remember the obstacles that you've already overcome in your life. Those were setbacks that you experienced but managed to get through.*

6. Distribute index cards with qualities that promote success (from the previous session). Ask students to display cards on the table in front of them.

7. Ask, *What are some possible challenges you might face as you move toward your goal? How will these qualities that are part of you help you successfully overcome those challenges? What will that look like?*

8. *What qualities would you like to develop because they seem like they would be useful as you move ahead?*

9. *Who is most likely to support you? What qualities do they have that you value?*

Ending

Final thought: *What can you do now that you might not have done or done as easily nine weeks ago?*

Express interest in how group members might support each other beyond the group experience.

Invite members to take the cards with the list of qualities that have helped them be successful and save them for reviewing at a later time or whenever they feel stuck about something.

SUMMARY

The group agendas in this chapter were created to demonstrate how principles from solution-focused brief counseling can be applied to groups. As a group leader, you have access to a massive collection of group activity books that will give you a framework to build on as you consider developing group agendas. The group leader does not need to begin from scratch and can piggyback on the good ideas of others. Most activities need a little adapting to be consistent with a solution-focused approach; Chapters 4 and 5 provided the structure to do just that.

CHAPTER NINE

Troubleshooting

Consultation is the gold standard for managing any practice issues in the mental health profession. This applies to practitioners in private practice, agencies, hospitals, and schools. When something is not working, do some troubleshooting with a colleague who understands both you and groups. The tendency for most of us is to do more of what we are already doing—only with more intensity, sometimes punitively, and usually with an edge that students pick up right away. Consultation is a great way to see the issue through someone else's eyes and, hopefully, see it differently. When the group of professionals with whom you work have a common understanding that you will all consult each other as needed, any hesitation that you have about bothering someone will dissipate.

POTENTIAL SNAGS

We will run into bumps on the road. The challenge is not the bumps—the challenge is doing something different when what we started with is not working. Some bumps in the road are more predictable than others. As you strategize on alternatives, your goal is to try something different; by now this may be your mantra! Following are some of the potential issues that snag many of us.

The Problem With Suggestions

Group counseling is an ideal setting for helping students come up with something different. The group has a wealth of ideas and experience. The participants end up helping each other as long as the leader stays out of the advice-giving business. Students get stumped by their own challenges; when the leader asks, *What have you tried?* the standard response is that they have tried everything. Leader alert: Do not say, *Well, what about* X*?* because *X* is sure to be a bad idea!

> *Well, what about* X*?* What solution-focused assumption does this ill-conceived question violate?

Ask instead if others in the group have run into something similar and, if so, how they handled it. If students are befuddled, the leader may need to come up with related situations to get the conversation going. Usually, someone has a situation that is related. This student may have tried a strategy that will work for the student with problem *X*.

Usually others join in, but let's assume they do not. The student with the *X* problem is stuck, and no one else can relate. The leader can express concern: *How have you managed as well as you have?* It may fit to ask, *What have you thought of that you ruled out; maybe there is something there to reconsider?* But it is also all right to defer the discussion to a later date. *This is a really difficult situation, and we are all stuck. Maybe we all need to think on it. Between now and the next meeting, how about paying attention to anything you notice that makes it work out even a little better and telling us what you noticed next week?* As leaders, we keep *asking* and we avoid *telling*. When we take this approach, there is no guarantee that students will come up with something different, but it is a sure bet that if we *tell* them what to do differently, the odds of it happening plummet!

Do You Really Need That Handout?

A classic mistake for beginning group leaders is to base the plan for the meeting around a handout the students will complete. There is something comforting for the leader about having a paper to hold on to as the group begins. But do you need it?

The goal is to get students to talk with *each other,* not to the paper. We want students to develop good communication skills and learn to relate to each other. We want them to listen and reflect back what they have heard. We want them to tolerate and understand differences. The paper task is only a prop, and you can usually get creative and skip that step.

Another issue with handouts is the close resemblance to homework. I have never encountered a student who said, *"Please, give me more homework."* You may lose the students before you get going if what you are asking them to do looks too much like school.

Adapting Material for Poor Readers

Another problem with tasks that require reading and writing is a possible lack of skills on the part of the students. No matter how competent you think the group is, it is good practice to have an idea of how to do the same activity without requiring the reading and writing part. You can easily be surprised that the very verbal boy has terrible spelling or the second-language learner who has great conversational skills reads several years below grade level. If the meeting you are in the middle of depends on a worksheet, and it is all set to fail, you may find yourself in an awkward situation.

Students will sometimes choose to act up rather than appear incompetent. We can innocently make students feel stupid when we rely too heavily on paper-and-pencil tasks. Always be prepared to adapt for kids who do not read and write well for their age, and use handouts cautiously. But beware that if we adapt material for one student, and the rest of the group does the task without help, we may have singled out deficits and caused embarrassment.

There is, however, a place for some pencil-and-paper tasks, and there are ways to modify handouts you think are spectacular. Here are some strategies to help with the handout you cannot give up:

1. Review the handout in the group and read it aloud before asking students to do anything.

2. Alter the vocabulary to ensure that it is at an early reading level.

3. Add pictures or simple sketches to the handout.

4. Ask someone who teaches English as a second language to review it. (These teachers are geniuses at modifying.)

Avoid Teaching Something

Some group leaders are former teachers and some are current teachers. While this background is a valuable asset in working with students, it is important to approach solution-focused group counseling as a leadership role quite separate from teaching.

When we function in a teaching role, we are most often in the expert position. When we function in a solution-focused capacity, we want the student to function as the expert. As noted earlier, asking a *how* question is a useful way to emphasize student expertise.

Some groups are specifically intended to teach a skill; these groups are called psycho-educational groups. While this kind of group serves a valuable function, this is not the kind of counseling group being discussed.

Here are a few tips for staying out of teacher territory. When we find our meeting plan sounding more like a lesson plan than a counseling meeting agenda, we are probably teaching. Noticing that we are standing in front of the group (and perhaps writing on the board) rather than sitting among the students is another possible alert that we have slipped into a teaching role. When we ask follow-up questions that start with, *What did you learn?* we may also be teaching.

There is a further refinement to this issue that merits attention. The younger the student, the more structure is required to have a positive group experience. The leader is more active with younger students than with older students. This can seem like teaching, but the skillful leader will ask questions and actively notice strengths without leading the younger students.

Goal Phobia

There may be students who either cannot formulate a goal or may be slow to develop one. In those cases it works to simply notice and build on strengths—goals may evolve over time. It is possible to have a group without all students developing specific personal goals, but after a couple of weeks it is helpful to ask, *How will we know at the end of these meetings that it was worth it for you to have spent the time talking to each other? What would you like to see be different as a result of trying to sort out these issues in your life?* Asking about a goal does not have to be stated as a goal; with some students, it is preferable to be indirect.

Groups to Avoid

Some kinds of groups are not a good fit for schools, even though most practitioners will get requests to provide these kinds of groups. Groups to avoid include ones with themes such as the following:

Bipolar disorder

Cutting behaviors

Eating disorders

Sexual abuse

This is not an exhaustive list, but these are the obvious clinical issues that require more intense services than can be provided at a school site. Additionally, in some areas, gang-related groups would not be safe to have on a school campus. Groups for students who are gay, lesbian, bisexual, or questioning their sexuality are sometimes requested. If the leader has training and experience with these issues, it is a possibility. As a preferred alternative, explore developing a Gay-Straight Alliance (GSA) club on campus. Since a counseling group implies there is a social-emotional issue that is problematic, it is better to attend to the needs of these groups from within a club as opposed to counseling environment. For information about this option, see www.glsen.org/cgi-bin/iowa/student/student/index.html.

With a request for any group, the critical question to ask ourselves is,

Does offering this kind of group fall within my training and experience?

This is an ethical issue and requires serious consideration. On occasion, we are asked to lead a group for which we have training but limited experience. In this case, if the topic is school appropriate, we might arrange for peer supervision, attend additional trainings, and read related literature and research as a way to prepare. A group that is outside our training and experience is a snag we can see coming and a problem we can avoid.

INTERVENTION IDEAS

In this section, there are ideas for intervening when students are distressed, something that happens with some frequency in counseling groups. Following this discussion are some ways to spruce up a group that seems to lack zest and sparkle.

Handling Crying and Grief

Avoid assuming that a student should cry because something is sad. A death in the family, or for young children the death of a pet, is usually a distressing event, but the first time a topic is broached may not be the time to actually talk about it. Sometimes a student will choose to say something brief about a huge issue just to test the waters, to see if it is safe to bring a difficult topic up later. If we pry too soon, or invite them to say too much too early, we risk having them feel exposed and potentially not returning to the group.

Sometimes, even though we try, there is no stopping a student who is bursting to share something that results in the overwhelmed student collapsing in a bucket of tears. We might have asked about something completely unrelated and still have gotten the tearful response. Moments like these call for masterful finesse. If we rush to comfort, and comfort too much, we may inadvertently give the message that the student cannot cope. Leaving the group to retrieve a box of tissues is, in my opinion, not a good idea either. This gives the message that we assume there is much more to say (which keeps the focus on the problem), and it breaks our contact with the group at an important moment. Students can easily sniffle for a bit!

> If the person sniffling is an adolescent boy, he is likely to be mortified, and handing him a tissue will only throw a spotlight on the problem. Even if there are tissues at hand, he is likely to use his sleeve: This behavior takes some of the perceived wimpiness out of the situation.

There are many effective ways to handle these kinds of situations. One way is to give the student some space to regain composure by saying, *It is easy to see how upsetting this issue is for you. And it is easy to see that you are really grappling with it. I wonder if you would like a moment to catch your breath and collect your thoughts before we go on. We could give other students a chance to talk for a moment about whether they have experienced anything similar or related. Would that fit with what you need at the moment?*

The decisions we make at important choice points such as this are related to the theoretical orientation that is our foundation. For example, from a psychodynamic perspective, healing is promoted when a student talks it out and processes the concern. Handling grief from an SFBC perspective is quite different. We might ask the students if they think it would help to talk about the loss and let them decide. If it would be helpful to talk about the loss, that is perfectly acceptable; this gives us an opportunity to strengthen our relationship. But rather than leave the conversation at that point, we might also initiate a conversation that focuses on the things the student has done to manage. A question that would fit would be something like, *Given all that you have been dealing with, how have you managed as well as you have?* Students love this kind of question, and as soon as they answer it, they are talking about strengths.

Increase the Cool Factor

Unless we are providing groups to all students in a school, students know they have been referred to us because there is a problem. This is like students knowing which reading group is the lowest in the class—students have good radar for this type of thing. Therefore, in all the ways in which we interact with students, our goal at a bare minimum is to *do no harm*. It would be regrettable if a student felt *more* of whatever issue was troubling him or her as a result of coming to the group: more rejected, less likable, more incompetent.

One way to minimize any negative affect associated with being in the group is to increase the coolness of being there. With little kids, this may mean using markers instead of crayons and adding stickers and sparkles. Younger kids love to role play. Most everyone enjoys an audience. Add video- or audiotaping and they will clamor to see it repeatedly. With older students, incorporate video or music clips—even photography—all this with the correct per-missions. A music clip makes a great conversation starter; teens have *lots* of opinions about music. Once you get them going, it is easier to redirect the conversation. For example, if you want to have a conversation about morals or ethics, start with Hollywood stars and bring magazine photos.

Create a Dilemma

Creating a dilemma for students to discuss is almost in the cool category as long as there is more than one way to resolve the issue and no obvious right answer. When there is only one correct resolution, students can feel like they are being lectured, even if subtly. As with all issues, start in tame territory. At the high school level in a group on peer pressure, you might ask, *What effect does swearing in songs, on TV, and in movies have on the language of youth today? Does it hurt or is it expressive? Does it make a difference? Do you think kids feel pressure to swear to be cool? What are effective ways to handle any pressure?* These questions may or may not be tame for your group, so evaluate appropriateness. Do not, however, start with, *Should Caucasian movie stars adopt kids of differing ethnicities?* This second question is far too loaded with potential landmines and may never be appropriate for a group. Let's look at this issue more closely.

Most classrooms with typically adjusted teens (is there such a thing?) would have a hard time with this second discussion topic. It is fair to assume that students who are referred to you are challenged in some way and may not yet have the resources to manage as well as peers. Teens may have strong feelings, even if the feelings are not necessarily connected to well-thought-out ideas. That makes it hard to have an informed discussion and really easy to have a fight. Avoid topics that will provoke these types of fights. Make the content match the developmental level of the group. We all want to end up looking good—like we know what we are talking about—even if we don't. It is simply good judgment to avoid putting students in situations where being passionate can lead down a sinkhole. The discussion question about adoption and race, and questions like it, are best left off the table in a group.

SELF-EVALUATION

As counselors, the essence of our role necessitates that we are self-reflective. We get repeated opportunities to step back and self-examine. Students will point out our flaws (whether we like it or not!), and we can choose not to be defensive. Student comments, even if haphazard, are a unique opportunity to rethink what we are doing, review our motivation and intentions, and then get creative. This useful process is closely related to maintaining an open attitude and staying out of the expert role.

Revealing Personal Information

It will not be long before some teenager in a group asks you if you ever tried drugs. Consider my prediction a gift! Giving some thought to how to handle this situation may save you from turning scarlet and stammering and then saying something you later regret. Putting the facts aside here, you are in a dilemma. If you say you have never done drugs, you may lose credibility and get categorized as someone who does not know what he or she is talking about. You may sound nerdy. If you say you have tried drugs, students may feel the boundary between adult and student slip away, and this can ultimately be unsettling to them. They may resent the adult/student boundary, but they count on it all the same. In addition, we can be perceived as overly aligned with students and lose our ability to maintain neutrality. It is also quite likely to get advertised around the school that you do drugs, and it will not be long before this juicy information gets to folks in high places. At the very least, you will have some explaining to do. So what do you do?

Whenever the issue of revealing personal information arises, the most important question to ask ourselves is, *What is in the best interest of the students?* The guiding principle is that any information revealed fosters something positive for students and is not just serving our needs. In the case of the drug question, the way to serve the best interest of the students is probably not to answer the question, no matter what the real answer is. There are, however, several ways to do this—and some avenues can be disastrous! Examine some possibilities below and consider what might work best.

1. I really don't think my personal life has any bearing on this conversation.

2. I don't really mind talking about myself, but I don't want to take the focus off you.

3. What do you imagine is my answer to this question?

4. I'd rather not talk about it.

All of these responses, even if worded differently, manage to achieve varying levels of absolutely *awful* as a response. They have great potential to make students irritated, overfocused on the leader, and argumentative. A preferred response is to simply be transparent and lay out the dilemma to students. It works well to say that you are in a no-win situation (adapted from T. Barnes, 2000, personal communication). Summon your best nondefensive voice and adapt the following idea. If you say you have not tried drugs, you look like a geek. If you say you have tried drugs, you have broken the law and this would be negative modeling. You can add that you get the question all the time and since it does not serve a positive purpose, you have decided that the best policy is not to answer the question. You can add an apology to soften the response, and then try to get back on track.

Inevitably, just when you feel triumphant at dodging this bullet and grateful that you had the good sense to come up with an answer, a student will say in an endearing way, *"Oh, c'mon, we aren't going to tell anyone, really. Just tell us. It will help us, really."* This may become a group chorus and will feel like an onslaught of persuasion. Expect it and be playful, but do not change your mind. A strength-based approach and a way to change the subject would be to admire their amazing skills of persuasion and ask questions like, *How did you get to be so persuasive? What do you think is your best approach? Who are you most successful with? How do you know when to not even try? Who would you say is your best model? What would you say is your least successful strategy?* The answer to all these questions (and others you may add) once again brings on an attack of expertise. They will talk about their strengths and their observations, and you may have managed to change the subject. Whew.

Check Your *Shoulds* at the Door

Clearly, we have expectations for student behavior and language that are school appropriate. These kinds of expectations generally hold true while running a group. However, expectations about how kids ought to be, what they ought to think, and what they should say can ruin a group and discourage a group leader who is left baffled and asking, *Where did it go wrong?* This is particularly an issue at the secondary level where the developmental task is to separate and individuate. "Should" ideas sneak into our minds unbidden. It starts with little things, such as *guys shouldn't have pierced ears.* Left unexamined and unchecked, these kinds of judgments can leak into more dangerous territory, such as *parents with children shouldn't get divorced.*

Sometimes we inherit them from our parents and can hear ourselves repeat the same shoulds as the previous generation. Sometimes those ideas are ones that hold up over time, such as *parents should not beat their children.* But many ideas do not hold up under close scrutiny. When we pay close attention, should statements are often statements about how someone else ought to be in order to meet our personal standards. They are judgments. Students on the other end of this judgment feel criticized and defensive. There is no way to have a successful group experience with this dynamic in the way. Consider the following example.

If the principal at the alternative high school asks you to do a group with the pregnant teens in the program, it would be wise to self-evaluate. If there are any shoulds lurking around, you have a choice: You can either refer the group to a colleague, or you can consult with someone you trust to help you assess your ideas and feelings more clearly. When we dust off the ideas and consciously examine them, shoulds will not lurk around and contaminate as easily.

If you hold the notion (even if you think you have it concealed) that these pregnant girls did something wrong or made a mistake, questions will fly out of your mouth that are less than therapeutic. An unfortunate question might sound like the following:

How do you feel about being pregnant again?

Did you use birth control?

Do you find you are making the same mistakes as your mother?

Would you be interested in hearing about how adoption works?

With each of these questions, there is an implied should. Most teens would respond to these questions like they were in a duck-and-cover exercise. This meeting might well be the last. The therapeutic conversation we intended to have cannot take place in this environment. There is an alternative: Closely examine your shoulds so they are less likely to become a destructive force. There is an old adage that fits here: "Healer, know thyself." The modern equivalent is "Consult, consult, consult."

Judgment

The kissing cousin of shoulds is judgment. Even when we think we have it concealed, it can wreck havoc. To illustrate this point, consider the following short story shared by author Chris Trout of Strengths in Focus (www.strengthsinfocus.com):

The Loaded Gun

I heard a wonderful story this week that I want to share, though I don't know its source. (I'm hoping maybe one of you will know its origins.)

Two researchers set off to study the same kind of gorillas in nearby parts of Africa. Both were highly skilled and successful animal researchers. Both spent hundreds of hours observing and studying the behavior of these magnificent beasts. Yet, when they wrote up their observations, it was as if they had been studying completely different species. The first researcher had been able to integrate with the gorillas, sitting amidst them and being invited into some of their customs and habits. The second had been unable to gain the trust of the gorillas, who remained fearful and distrusting of his presence.

Intrigued, they dug deeper. Both knew and used the same techniques and strategies. Both were insightful and experienced. They could identify only one significant variable that was different. The second researcher had a gun. It stayed hidden in his bag and he didn't carry it with him. Yet the gorillas reacted as if he were carrying it in plain sight.

Was the gun simply the symbol of a subtle sense of fear and distrust that the second researcher carried into the field? Is this what the gorillas perceived?

There is little doubt in my mind. I have seen this at work over and over, most clearly in a teen center where my windowed office had a full view of "floor." I had carefully recruited and trained 35 wonderful volunteers. Fifteen minutes into the first day, I looked out to see two volunteers who looked, for all intents and purposes, like they were doing the same thing. The kids were telling one (repeatedly) to "f-off," while the other was being entrusted with stories about the kids' lives as they played pool together.

Same strategies. Same techniques. One had a "gun" (judgment) in his bag, the other didn't. The kids knew.

Man, did they know.

Like it or not, in the end it all starts with our intent, doesn't it?

SOURCE: Chris Trout. (2008). *Strengths in Focus.* Strengths Ezine. www.strengthsinfocus.com

This compelling story is a powerful example of the force of our thoughts. We cannot hide! Our thoughts reveal themselves in unintended ways. Left unexamined, thoughts can wreak havoc on our good intentions. Fortunately, thoughtful self-reflection helps us get the gun out of our bag.

Listening Loudly

We cannot listen loudly when we are fired up about an idea or a strategy. As dedicated professionals, there is a tendency to want to fix things, an urgent desire to make children's lives better. This desire can propel us into quicksand.

Let's imagine that you do everything you can to set up a group in a way that maximizes the odds that your group will be successful. You have a good plan with built-in flexibility. The plan is grounded in a theoretical orientation that makes sense for your group. The selection of the members has been done with an eye for a good balance of strengths in the group, and you have strong teacher and parent support. You are excited about this group and eagerly anticipate the first meeting.

Then something bad happens. At the first meeting, you notice (but cannot stop) that you are *talking too much*. You are so anxious to put your plan into action that you hurry and interrupt. The thought of a few minutes of silence feels terrifying, and you find yourself filling too many spaces in the conversation. Under this kind of self-imposed pressure, it becomes exceedingly difficult to really listen to what students have to say. The trick is to slow down, breathe, and have faith in the group process. The odds are that most of the students want to be there, even if to save face they act as if this was their last choice behind picking up garbage in the halls. Usually students are curious. The younger kids want to know what you will do, and the teens want to know what other students will say. In both cases, this works for you as the leader. The trick is to stay in the leadership role without taking over the conversation. The only way to do this is to listen loudly.

Manage Your Own Energy

One day, I noticed I was a better listener when allergies were bothering me. It was an odd revelation. As a high-energy person, it occurred to me that with my energy a bit dampened, I was more effective. When my allergies were acting up, I was actually doing a better job of attending—not thinking ahead so much, not creating my next question before the person fully responded, and remembering what was said. Energy and enthusiasm are good qualities, *and* they may require some taming in order to channel that energy in the most effective way for a group. Modulating your energy to match the needs of the group has one striking result: Managing your energy improves listening ability exponentially.

Don't Blame the Kids: Get More Creative

Many years ago, Steve deShazer (1985) took the shocking position that there was no such thing as a resistant client. At the time, a client was considered resistant when there was no therapeutic progress, no change; this was a mainstream notion in the dominant psychodynamic model. In contrast, deShazer believed that blaming the client for lack of progress was misguided. Instead of blaming the client, the therapeutic obligation is to get more creative, try something different, and stay curious.

In the school setting, when our desire to help students is frustrated, the blame-the-student response erupts without notice. Blaming the parents is a related phenomenon, as is blaming the system. The trouble with any of these approaches is that we do not figure out what to do differently by focusing our energy on blaming, which is the equivalent of giving up. Blaming is an energy vampire. We burn up energy and we burn out in the end, and we have wasted precious time that could be spent on creating possibilities.

Making Genuine Apologies

The gnawing feeling that translates into *I wish I hadn't said that* seems to be a by-product of our normal imperfection and presents us with an opportunity to continue to refine our skills (pretty good reframe!). Continuous apologizing is not recommended, but there are times when a sincere apology is appropriate. Most students are so unaccustomed to being on the receiving end of an apology that it usually catches them by surprise. This can be an effective way to model behaviors and values that are consistent with a solution-focused approach. It might sound like this:

I've thought a lot about something that happened in our meeting last week, and I've decided that I want to make an apology to all of you. I so regret teasing about something that may not be funny to all of you. It was insensitive of me and a misjudgment on my part. I regret that it happened, and I will pay closer attention to this kind of thing in the future. I just wanted to say that before we go on today. Does anyone want to add anything? If not, we'll move on with the plan for today. I just wanted to clear the air before we start. Again, my apologies.

The power of this kind of statement is connected to the infrequency with which it is used. If self-doubt creeps up on us or we have an attack of self-criticism, repeated apologies are not the solution. Sometimes our best strategy is to accept our minimistakes, learn from the situation, and move on. The good news is we are self-monitoring and attending to what does not work; the better news is that we *will* come up with something different.

SUMMARY

Challenges are predictable, some more than others. Peer consultation is one of the most effective ways to strategize about solutions. The main theme of the chapter can be summarized in this way: If what you are doing is not working, at least *do something different!*

In this chapter, we examined three specific ways to troubleshoot: analyze the presentation of the material, consider alternative interventions, and self-monitor. Several typical snags seen in group counseling were discussed. Intervention strategies that attend to specific needs and can add sparkle to the group were considered. Last, many forms of self-monitoring were described.

CHAPTER TEN

The Power of Groups

W e can accomplish things in a group that are often out of reach when students are seen individually. Peer feedback can be a jumpstart for change, and the group experience provides opportunities for generalization of skills. Students may bumble around or come up with odd ideas, but in the end, most manage to add to the group experience. Very few students are just downright mean. When they offer "support" to each other, they can sound like that family member we all have who says *exactly* (perhaps tactlessly) what he thinks without editing a syllable. Somehow it works out most of the time. Students are curious about each other, and this works in favor of creating and sustaining an effective group process.

THE STUDENTS

Students have exquisite radar for adults who genuinely believe in them and see their potential. Younger students are hungry for acknowledgment and the opportunity to show us what they know and can do. Secondary students can go to great lengths using their nonchalance to convince us they do not care! Regardless of the presentation, the need system is the same. Students want to be seen and understood. We can meet this need individually, but when we lead a group, the opportunity for each student to be seen and understood increases exponentially.

Believing in Students

Consider two well-known examples of teachers who fiercely believed in their students. Erin Gruwell's first teaching assignment in the 1990s was with a culturally diverse high school group of so-called unteachable delinquents in Long Beach, California (Freedom Writers & Gruwell, 1999). Her class went from being written off to writing and publishing a book called *The Freedom Writers Diary*. The compelling story of this group's transformation was made into a movie of the same name in 2007 and starred an Academy Award–winning actress.

The story is powerful because the unbeatable combination of believing in students and helping them develop the skills they needed was the ticket to a new life. These students wrote about "gangs, immigration, drugs, violence, abuse, death, anorexia, dyslexia, teenage love, weight issues, divorce, suicide" (www.freedomwritersfoundation.org). On the Freedom Writers' Foundation Web site, students talk about Room 203 as "our safe haven, where we could cry, laugh, and share our stories without being judged." It was a tumultuous journey for both the teacher and the students, but when these students became a *group*, what opened up before them was a universe where all things were possible—a long way from the racial hostility and poor academic performance that had entrapped them not long before. At first, these students had only one person who believed in them: their teacher. Over time, they grew to believe in themselves. The list of believers grew until it included the whole nation via major network television interviews, a book, and a movie. The applause continues.

Other student groups have had public acclaim for achieving what was thought to be impossible. A high school math teacher, Jaime Escalante, believed that Mexican American students in Los Angeles's poorest schools could take accelerated math classes that lead to Advanced Placement calculus and college credit. He started with five students in 1978; by 1980, he taught thirty-two calculus students. Eight years later, just under 450 students had taken the AP exam and more than 50 percent passed. The dropout rate at Garfield High was 55 percent in 1978; by 1988 it was only 14 percent. This story became the movie *Stand and Deliver*. It is another testament to what students can do when others believe in them and they learn to believe in themselves.

To accomplish great things, we must not only act, but also dream; not only plan, but also believe.

Anatole France

Success Breeds Success

Students in these two classes had life-altering experiences. In both cases, someone believed in the students, worked with them as a group, and helped them develop the skills they needed. These are the key dynamics of a successful solution-focused counseling group. While the in-the-trenches work that goes on quietly in school counseling groups will not often win Academy Awards, the contribution to the lives and futures of students is immeasurable all the same.

> *It is literally true that you can succeed best and quickest by helping others to succeed.*
>
> Napoleon Hill

THE PROCESS

Having a solid grasp of a theoretical orientation allows for "degrees of freedom" from a formulaic approach. We can lead more skillfully with the assurance that we know where we are headed—even if the road to get there has twists and turns. We can be in charge without having to be overcontrolling and can trust in students' ability to change. The net sum is that we can believe in the process, and students will experience us as believing in them.

The Fix-It Trap

Group counseling is a powerful force for positive change when used wisely in a school setting. Even so, working in groups with students is not a panacea. We will still have evenings where we go home downhearted and say to ourselves, *If I could just . . .* We may have a miracle question, but we are limited in the make-a-miracle department. We are often asked to help kids through the most complex and horrific situations, problems no students should have to deal with—and yet they do. We must be prepared to meet those needs as effectively as we can. Our greatest power to improve the lives and relationships of the students in our care is to be skillful at empowering them, to teach them to fish instead of giving them a fish, and to help them see their resourcefulness and strengths.

This Sounds Like a Lot of Work!

It's true. Adapting activities to make them solution focused takes time at the start, but the initial investment does lead to time savings. Group agendas can be used repeatedly. In addition, many individual activities are great for any group, no matter what the theme. A good group introductory activity may work as well for a divorce group as it does for a friendship group. Many of the activities that work for an anger management group would be fine for a group on ADHD. We can mix and match as we adapt material. As a leader, it is fascinating to see groups respond so differently to the same activity; repetition does not bring on a case of leader boredom.

There is an economy of scale in seeing students in groups. Many agencies and health maintenance organizations that provide counseling services for adults and children now offer groups almost exclusively. We can see six students for 45 minutes in a group or six students individually for 45 minutes, and in the second case we have spent nearly five hours! If we assume the leader needs an hour of planning, we have still saved many hours when those six students are seen as a group.

Turning Individual Referrals Into a Group

School referrals to the counselor do not arrive by theme. We do not always have a way to group a student who has had a death in the family with others who have had the same experience. However, when we promote groups and when the faculty at a school site understands the referral system, we will have more opportunities to serve students as a group. The typical school counselor ends up with a waiting list of students to see. Rather than think of this as a waiting list for individual service, why not think of this list as a minigroup in the making? The students waiting for individual attention may wait no longer than the next group that is forming. Build it and they will come!

There will always be some students who are better suited to an individual approach. However, as counselors, we seem more likely to err in overemphasizing the individual approach. We typically get more training in individual work, so it is only logical that we gravitate to one-on-one counseling. This pull to individual counseling can eventually become a habit that is hard to break unless we stay attuned to how we think change occurs. As discussed at length in Chapter 1, if the change we are seeking is more likely to occur in a group, then offering a group is in the student's best interest.

THE LEADER

When we lead groups with a theoretical orientation as a basis for our interactions with students, we decrease the chances that the unexpected will unnerve us. Even with a solid group agenda, much of the interaction in any group is spontaneous. Skilled leaders are nimble and quick-witted. Students are active, unpredictable, and captivating, and the ideas and feelings they share warrant a flexible approach. It is possible to lead groups by whipping out a prepared group curriculum and following it much like the novice cook adheres to a recipe. But this approach will backfire eventually as the leader will be unprepared for the unexpected.

Misguided Self-Talk!

The hard part is *not* acknowledging that the dynamics of a group can accelerate change. Most of us can accept that this is at least a possibility. The hard part for most of us is moving out of our comfort zone and trying something that is unfamiliar and perhaps a bit intimidating.

To ward off the distressing feeling of *I can't*, let's make a list of all the things that might slow us down if we decide to up our commitment to group counseling. This is not, strictly speaking, very solution focused, but airing these fears may give us a laugh and help take the hot air out of the distortions. To create this completely unscientific list, an inventory of self-talk over the span of my career was all that was required!

The language of *I can't*:

- Sounds great, but I really don't have time.
- If someone would tell me what not to do so I'd have time to do groups, I'd be thrilled.
- OK, bottom line: I'm afraid I'll make a fool of myself.

- My reputation is good as is. I don't want someone walking by the room to hear kids yelling or swearing; it would be humiliating.
- Why embarrass myself by having kids say things that might make me paralyzed with indecision. I won't know what to do.
- I like these ideas; I just don't think I could do it. It's not my style.

We all have these not-so-helpful thoughts. Even those of us who went on to lead many groups had these thoughts. From a solution-focused perspective, how will you acknowledge these thoughts but not let them get in the way? How will you appreciate that what you may want to do is more important than the concern about doing it perfectly from the start? How will you keep your thoughts from interfering as you try something new? What will be your first small step?

A Career That Goes the Distance

When a good idea sprouts, it has a chance of becoming important to us if we nurture it. This is so obvious that it may sound preposterous—but think again. If you are already a working professional, you may have had this experience. You drag yourself to a conference hoping for an infusion of inspiring ideas, and in fact, that is exactly what happens. You delight in thinking about new ideas, you relate to colleagues, and you remember why you chose this career many years ago. You return to work invigorated, but you quickly deflate, playing catch up after your time away. Those great ideas fade from memory, and your more pressing goal now is to stay afloat. The handouts from those great workshops become another pile. The best of intentions are swept away as we find ourselves repeating what we have always done, whether it really works or not. If this sounds even mildly familiar, take careful note: It is a perfect plan for burnout.

If group counseling is on the verge of becoming an important idea to you, what is *one small step* you might take to nurture that idea? Maybe you'd like to read more about solution-focused approaches or seek out a conference or training. Perhaps it would be helpful to make a commitment with a colleague to have lunch or meet for coffee after work once a month to talk about how to implement groups at your site. One of the best ways to avoid job burnout is to see results, to see that what we do makes a difference—to see change.

We can invest more time and energy in learning new things when we see preliminary results spurred on by the enthusiasm of others.

> *In everyone's life, at some time, the inner fire goes out. It is then burst into flame by an encounter with another human being. We should all be thankful for those people who rekindle the inner spirit.*

Albert Schweitzer

Uncommon Heroes With a Common Purpose

There are some traits that, if nurtured, make any group leader better: a sense of humor, flexibility, good organization and planning, curiosity, and an ability to laugh at ourselves. Other qualifications for the job of group leader include good training (even if it was designed by you), consultation, and a dedication to continuing education.

A sense of adventure is also an asset for a group leader. Running groups in the schools is definitely an adventure. Your adventure. Your job description. Your chance to make a difference in the lives of young people. Isn't that exactly why you got into this profession?

> *Never doubt that a small group of thoughtful, committed citizens can change the world; indeed, it's the only thing that ever has.*

Margaret Mead

References

Anhar, J., Crisp-Handleson, A., Grove, B., & Zehnder, N. (2006). *What's the hype?* Unpublished manuscript, Sacramento State, Sacramento, CA.

Asay, T. P., & Lambert, M. J. (1999). The empirical case for the common factors in therapy: Quantitive findings. In M. A. Hubble, B. L. Duncan, & S. D. Miller (Eds.), *The heart and soul of change: What works in therapy* (pp. 33–56). Washington, DC: American Psychological Association.

deShazer, S. (1985). *Keys to solution in brief therapy.* New York: W. W. Norton.

deShazer, S. (1988). *Clues: Investigating solutions in brief therapy.* New York: W. W. Norton.

Dubitsky, M., Macias, G., & Quintero, C. (2007). *Friendship club.* Unpublished manuscript, Sacramento State, Sacramento, CA.

Durrant, M. (1995). *Creative strategies for school problems.* New York: W. W. Norton.

Freedom Writers & Gruwell, E. (1999). *How a teacher and 150 teens used writing to change themselves and the world around them.* New York: Broadway Books.

Furman, B., & Ahola, T. (1992). *Solution talk: Hosting therapeutic conversations.* New York: W. W. Norton.

Gingerich, W. J., & Eisengart, S. (2000). Solution-focused brief therapy: A review of the outcome research. *Family Process, 39,* 477–498.

Gottman, J. (1995). *Why marriages succeed or fail: And how you can make yours last.* New York: Fireside.

Haley, J. (1973). *Uncommon therapy.* New York: W. W. Norton.

LaFountain, R. (1993). Trends that differentiate school counselors regarding burnout. *The Pennsylvania Counselor, 39,* 20–21.

LaFountain, R., & Garner, N. E. (1998). *A school with solutions: Implementing a solution-focused/Adlerian-based comprehensive school counseling program.* Alexandria, VA: American School Counselor Association.

LaFountain, R., Garner, N. E., & Eliason, G. T. (1996). Solution-focused counseling groups: A key for school counselors. *School Counselor, 43,* 256–267.

Metcalf, L. (2008). *The field guide to counseling towards solutions: The solution-focused school.* San Francisco: Jossey-Bass.

Murphy, J. J. (2008). *Solution-focused counseling in schools.* Alexandria, VA: American Counseling Association.

O'Hanlon, W., & Weiner-Davis, M. (1987). *In search of solutions: A new direction in psychotherapy* (2nd ed.). New York: W. W. Norton.

Parsad, B., Alexander, D., Farris, E., & Hudson, L. (2004). High school guidance counseling. *Education Statistics Quarterly, 5.* Retrieved March 13, 2008, from http://nces.ed.gov/programs/quarterly/Vol_5/5_3?3_4.asp

Seligman, M. E. P., & Csikszentmihalyi, M. (2000). Positive psychology: An introduction. *American Psychologist, 55,* 5–14.

Sklare, G. (2005). *Brief counseling that works.* Thousand Oaks, CA: Corwin Press.

Steen, S., Bauman, S., & Smith, J. (2007). Professional school counselors and the practice of group work. *Professional School Counseling, 11,* 72–80.

Trout, C. (2008, February 11). The loaded gun. *Strengths in Focus Newsletter,* Retrieved July 30, 2008, from http://community.icontact.com/p/strength_sinfocus/newsletters/strengths_ezine/posts/strengths-ezine-a-gun-in-your-bag

Vernon, A. (2006). *Thinking, feeling, behaving: An emotional education curriculum for children.* Champaign, IL: Research Press.

Walter, J. L., & Peller, J. E. (1992). *Becoming solution-focused in brief therapy.* New York: Brunner/Mazel.

Weiner-Davis, M., deShazer, S., & Gingerich, W. J. (1987). Building on pre-treatment change to construct a therapeutic solution. *Journal of Marital and Family Therapy, 13,* 359–363.

Index

CORWIN
A SAGE Company

The Corwin logo—a raven striding across an open book—represents the union of courage and learning. Corwin is committed to improving education for all learners by publishing books and other professional development resources for those serving the field of PreK–12 education. By providing practical, hands-on materials, Corwin continues to carry out the promise of its motto: **"Helping Educators Do Their Work Better."**